From Within

Let your
Light Shine
Brightly!

FROM WITHIN

My Path of Hope and Healing from Sexual Abuse

BY GIGI KILROE

Published by InsideOut Press, January 2022

www.gigikspeaks.com

Cover design: Denise Daub
Interior design: Veronica Daub

ISBN-13: 978-0-9992111-4-4
Library of Congress Control Number: 2021902487
First Edition
Printed in the United States of America

I would like to dedicate this book to survivors of incest, dating violence, and sexual assault. May you each find happiness and peace as you travel your journey to healing. I want you know this: **No one** has the right to extinguish the light that shines within you.

ACKNOWLEDGMENTS

I definitely would not be the woman I am today without the help and guidance of my therapist, Leigh Calloway. I do believe there are angels on earth because she is one of them. She believed in me and I trusted her completely. I would have not been able to walk this journey of healing without her support.

To my amazing lifelong friends, you each mean the world to me. Even through my darkest times, your love and laughter kept me going. Thank you for being in my life!

A huge thank you to my team of amazing peer reviewers for this book. Your help was incredible: Mari Donnelly, Leigh Calloway, Wendy Ripley, Janet Hayden, Charlotte Myers, Maggie Rymsza, Cindy Young, Dawn Muchow and, especially, Eileen Sparduti. I adore each of you; your insight has been invaluable.

To my goddaughter Chrissy, I love you more than I can ever put into words. Thank you for all the joy you bring to my life.

And a very special thank you to Kim Olver, whose support and commitment in helping me share my journey and message is beyond a gift. I will be forever grateful.

Contents

“I have been many women in my lifetime.
I have been the protector and provider.
I have been the lover and the fighter,
but the woman within I value the most,
will always be the survivor.”

– S.L. Heaton

THE GODDESS

$\mathcal{I}$ was 5 years old on that November night in 1965. My dad had tears in his eyes when he asked me to come into my parents' bedroom and sit down. My dad stood 6'1" tall, nearly 300 pounds, a gentle giant who had a heart the size of Texas, the greatest sense of humor and jovial laugh of anyone I have ever known. His joy and positive outlook were contagious. He had the most beautiful, kind, clear green Irish eyes that always seemed to sparkle, but that night, I saw they reflected horrific pain and loss. It was the first time I had ever seen my dad cry. For whatever reason, my attention went to the bold pink and maroon flowered print of their bedspread which looked so ugly to me. Then he said it, the words that forever changed my world, "Your mom is gone." I immediately looked up to my left out their window and couldn't take my eyes off the full moon. It seemed to take up the whole space of the window. Huge tears fell from his eyes. I was numb; I didn't understand. Where does someone go when they die? Was she now on that huge bright moon I kept staring at?

> "Bambi has a profound effect on children
> because it's about losing your mother."
> – Christine Baranski

She had been in and out of the hospital for as long as I could remember. She was diagnosed with lung cancer just 18 months prior. She was only 38 years old that November night... the night death stole her from me.

Back in 1965, it was not common for young children to

1

be allowed to visit patients in the hospital. Dad took me to see her a few days prior to that night. He was wearing his khaki-colored London Fog raincoat, which I hid under as we approached the elevator. We pretended to the other people that he was sneaking me in. I laughed and giggled, as a five year old would, not knowing the significance of this visit.

The nurses with her were so sweet. They told me I had been allowed to visit because the picture I had drawn for my mom was so special. When I walked into the room, she was in a bed that was on the left, not far from the window. There were long, skinny, green tubes coming from both of her nostrils, leading to a huge oxygen tank on the wall. She was frail, weak and almost unrecognizable. She looked so old to me. Her skin was a strange color, and she seemed to struggle to breathe. Her eyes that were once so lively and gorgeous were now dark, empty and hollow.

My mother had always been the epitome of class and fashion. She stood 6 feet tall, with short jet black naturally curly hair and stunning hazel eyes. She carried herself with such grace. I rarely remember a day that she was not impeccably dressed from head to toe. Three-inch heels, red lips, bold accessories and perfectly polished nails. Dresses, skirts, long white gloves, and always, always a matching purse. I would often explore her bracelets, trying them on in an attempt to emulate her majestic presence and beauty. I was fascinated by them. So huge on my little wrist, but sheer perfection on hers. She was a movie star and a goddess to me, and I wanted to be her.

Photographs are snapshots of a moment in time we never get back. I'm so grateful that my dad took so many photos and slides. Throughout the years I have spent endless hours looking at them, trying to imagine who she truly was. I study her face, her expressions, and her stance. I wish I knew what her voice sounded like, what her perfume smelled like, what made her laugh. All my life I've been told I look just like her.

I feel such love when I look at my favorite photo of my mom and me together. We are standing in front of our 1963 white Mercury convertible. She is wearing a straight black and white polka dot skirt that falls a few inches below the knee, black sleeveless top, black high heels, and sunglasses. Her scarf is wrapped fashionably around her head and her red lipstick accents her gentle smile. At the end of her elbow-length, white glove, she is holding my little hand. The smile on my face shows the happiness and innocence of an almost four-year-old child, whose hand is being held by the person she loves most in the world. It had been a beautiful sunny day. The color of my blue shorts outfit with a smiling clown and three balloons sewn on the front of my top matched the blue rim of my little sunglasses. Petite white ankle socks, white patent leather shoes with a side buckle and a white tie on the top of my head all complete my outfit. I am standing just in front of her, we both have our right leg a bit ahead of our left. Together we look like we are getting ready to take off on a journey. The smiling beaming little girl in that photo couldn't have known she'd be traveling life's journey without her mom.

The year I turned 38 was a tough one for me. Her life ended at that age, but I have had so many more years than she was robbed of. Many rough life lessons lay ahead for me, and I had to learn, grow, and heal them without her in my life. I can't even begin to imagine what her emotions were, knowing she was leaving her 5-year-old daughter behind.

> *"I'll never stop missing her,*
> *because I'll never stop loving her."*
> *– Grief to Hope with Nikki Pennington*

My mother had a brother that I had never met. I've only seen one photo of him. He was incredibly handsome, but it wasn't a kind face. Something about his eyes pierced right through me. I had an uncomfortable feeling each time I saw his photo in the old, brown, musty smelling, photo album. I couldn't have been more than 4 years old when a phone call came in that was terribly frightening, and it has never left my memory.

I was sitting on the floor playing with my dolls in the doorway of my parent's room. My mom was resting in bed when the phone rang. She picked it up and within just a few seconds, suddenly burst into tears. My dad flew past me and went storming in. He took the phone from her; I never saw him so furious. I was so frightened, not understanding what's happening.

My dad was shouting into the phone then slammed it down. I saw him clench his right hand into a fist and pound it into his left palm. At that moment those gentle Irish eyes were enraged. That right hand of his was mimicking punching into his palm... and hard. He grabbed his coat and hat and headed for the door. My mom was crying and begging, "John, don't!"

The call came from my mom's brother. I knew, even at that tender age, something was horribly wrong. Years later, I asked my dad about that night, but he only gave me small bits of information. I could tell it was painful for him to talk about. There had to have been some kind of abuse. My gut told me it had been either physical or sexual. It would be years later, while revisiting that memory on a hot July afternoon, when repressed trauma within me surfaced.

"There is something about losing your mother that is permanent and inexpressive—a wound that will never quite heal."
– Susan Wiggs

I was confused by the long green tubes, not quite sure what to make of them. The oxygen tank emitted a sound that I found unnerving. It looked to me like something I had seen on TV. I stared at it and it frightened me. They brought in a tray of food for her. The nurse lifted the lid off and the plate held turkey, gravy, mashed potatoes, white bread, milk and some kind of dessert. My mom took a couple sips of milk, a bite of bread and that was it. The next moments marked the pivotal beginning of my eating disorder.

My 5-year-old self thought that if I ate everything on her tray, it would make her better. I don't think I even chewed most of it, more like inhaled it. In what only felt like seconds, I had eaten every speck of food on that tray. I was physically beyond stuffed. The thing I remember most was that as I felt full physically, I felt numb emotionally. From that moment through the next 50-plus years, I learned that was my way to handle emotions. It became my coping mechanism. This visit on that cold November afternoon was the last time I would ever see her.

> *"I wish God didn't need you in heaven,*
> *because I need you here."*
> *– Unknown*

It was a closed casket at her funeral. I cried and carried on that I wanted to see her. I remember they opened the casket. The funeral director came up behind me and lifted me up so I could look into the casket. It hurt under my arms as he lifted me. To this day, I can see the pink flowers around the head of the casket, but when I go to look in... nothing. My mind has blocked it. It is not uncommon for children to block out incredibly painful memories and trauma, and for me, this was sadly just one example.

She was buried at Arlington National Cemetery. My only memory is looking out the window as the car was heading to the grave site. The hills and hills of white gravestones so perfectly spaced and aligned seemed to go on forever. The piercing blue color of the sky that day is burned in my memory. I looked to that blue sky. Where was she?

My parents, myself, and my half-brother (whom I'll refer to as HB) were living in an apartment outside of Washington, DC. My mother had been married before and my HB was 13 when I was born. Our apartment was decorated with her artwork and beautiful antiques. The Queen Ann chair and marble tables were gorgeous. She loved to paint and had replicated Japanese symbols that represented each of the four seasons. The background was gold, the letters in bold black, with slight shadings in red and white. Her creation hung on a vertical wood block that caught your eye as soon as you entered our downstairs apartment.

The Christmas before she passed, I can recall what looked like hundreds of strands of silver tinsel that softly dangled from the branches of the large tree, which was placed in the dining room just in front of the china hutch. I vividly remember all the furniture, plants and bookcases. Our black-and-white television with rabbit ears was positioned at an angle, coming from the right-hand corner in front of the large picture window. The apartment had a small narrow kitchen, stove on the left, refrigerator on the right. I had been given an Easy Bake oven as a gift. This was a working toy oven which first premiered in 1963. I loved its bright turquoise color. Perhaps my love for that color to this day is tied to a loving memory of my mom. I remember her helping me bake something for my dad. It's funny, I remember her giggling when I thought you were supposed to add everything from the refrigerator into that tiny baking pan. Perhaps the reason this memory is so vivid is because it's one of the last I have of her. Cancer robbed me of all those experiences that a mother and daughter are supposed to share. It's a never-ending open wound that, most times, is covered by a tissue-thin shield... but an emotional wave comes out of nowhere, ripping open the vulnerable emotions once again.

Next to the kitchen was the bathroom, the commode and sink were on the left, the large bathtub on the right. What I have absolutely no memory of, however, is where I slept.

Finishing first grade after her passing is a blur. But in the middle of one night in June 1966, my dad put all my things in the car, with a small U-Haul attached to the back, and we drove to my grandmother's (his mother) in Pennsylvania. I was focused on his loading my small ivory plastic vanity and chair and the navy blue and silver baby carriage that I loved. Pennsylvania would now be my home. He completely cut ties with my HB. This was completely uncharacteristic of my dad. I never understood why. Years later, it would all unfold.

The little girl on the front of this book is me. I clearly recall what I was thinking when my aunt snapped that photo. I was looking up to the sky wondering where my mom was. Was she up there in that never-ending blue sky? Could she see me?

When you place my high school senior photo next to my mom's, you can see an uncanny resemblance. We have the exact same expression on our faces. I have my dad's nose, but every other feature is my mom's. There is no doubt I look just like her. I always saw her beauty, but could never see my own.

When I was in my 30s, I discovered a wonderful book, *Motherless Daughters,* by Hope Edelman. I always keep a copy on hand. Now, as my friends are each beginning to lose their moms, I give them a copy of this book.

There are some things you never get over; you just learn to live around them. Sadly, I will never know what our relationship could or would have been like. She remains a goddess in my mind, with an elegant air of mystery.

For those of us who lost our mothers at an early age, we are members of a club that none of us want to belong to.

Since 1965 I have been, and will always be, a motherless daughter.

> *"When death takes your mother,*
>   *it steals that word forever."*
>   *– Mitch Albom*

GRAM

The house where I lived with my grandmother, in my heart, will always be home. It's amazing to me that my grandmother was 72 years old when I went to live with her. It's incredible that she took on the task of raising a 5 year old. I adored her. She was not demonstrative, but I knew she absolutely loved me. I'd say, "I love you, Gram," she'd always respond, "It's reciprocal." To this day, when I end a conversation by either phone or text with childhood friends, inevitably one will say, "I love you," the other responds, "It's reciprocal."

My mother's medical bills were astronomical. At the time of her illness, my dad did not have health insurance. He worked as a heavy construction superintendent and had the opportunity to work overseas to pay off the enormous debt he was left with. I certainly understood his decision and I never felt resentment towards him for temporarily leaving the country. I loved him so very much. He smelled of Old Spice aftershave and always had a cigar jutting from the right side of his mouth. His black glasses case always protruded from his left shirt pocket. He proudly wore his Columbia University college ring on his left ring finger. His brand of cigar was Dutch Masters. He would always let me have the cardboard box they came in. I loved to fill it with trinkets and crayons. Every time I would open the box, a faint whiff of cigar emerged. I loved it because it smelled like my dad. I thought the six men on the front of the box were Pilgrims. They had long loose brown tops, huge white collars and what I thought were Pilgrim hats.

To this day, one of my favorite photos of my dad shows him and my two cousins standing on my gram's porch. His size, sweater, hat and cigar would put you in mind of John Candy in the movie, *Uncle Buck*. Classic.

My Dad was mostly bald, and would perspire leaving large beads of sweat on the top of his head. I would snuggle up next to him on our long green couch, gently patting those beads with a Kleenex. That gesture always made me feel so close to him. Perhaps in my little mind, I was doing something to comfort him.

My parent's love story is so tender. He told me that on their first date, he told her he was going to marry her. That was December, and just two months later in February, they married on her 30th birthday. All his life he said to me, "Gi, you'll just know."

For several years, he came back to the states about twice a year. I would break out in hives before he got home. I was so excited and, apparently, my little nervous system reacted. There was a beautiful spot in the town called Irving Cliff. You could drive to the top and walk to an area that looked out over the whole town. It held a huge lighted star that when lit at night, could be seen for miles. When he would return from his travels, the first thing he would do was take me up to the cliff. It was one of his favorite places in the world and I treasured that time there with him. He truly was my hero. Years later, the term "hero" would have more meaning than I could have ever possibly imagined.

My gram was a little Irish woman who stood about 5'3" and always wore a dress. Her stockings were attached by clips at the bottom of her girdle. She kept a Kleenex tucked in her belt or up her sleeve. When she had to blow her nose, she only used one hand. I was fascinated by this, and one day I asked her why she did that. Her response was, "A lady only uses one hand."

My dad definitely inherited those sparkling, clear, green

Irish eyes, as well as her sense of humor. She was, however, a worrier. One day she said, "Oh dear." When I asked her what was wrong, she replied, "I have nothing to worry about."

She had her housedress for the mornings when she did household chores; then after lunch, she changed into a nicer dress. She had to be ready when *As the World Turns,* a soap opera, came on at 1:30 p.m. Her next favorite was *Another World,* which came on at 3 p.m. Her friends knew not to call her when her soaps were on. She was annoyed when the TV stations interrupted programming on the day of man's first steps on the moon. She had her routines!

Dinner was at 5 p.m. each night—no exceptions. Dinner had to be finished, dishes washed and put away by 5:30 p.m. because the TV show, The Jokers Wild, came on at 6 p.m. Every night before she went to bed, she'd put a teaspoon of Taster's Choice instant coffee in a cup and leave the spoon in it. It sat on the counter in the kitchen in the same exact place every night. I asked her one time why she did that, and she replied, "It saves time in the morning."

She always helped me with my homework. She was a whiz in math. She could add columns of numbers in her head. Her strength in math is definitely something I did NOT inherit. My biggest struggle was with reading. The district I was in for first grade focused on learning whole words. When I entered second grade in Pennsylvania, I didn't have a grasp on phonics. Learning how to sound out words was a huge challenge for me. I remained in the lowest reading group for several years. I thought I wasn't smart. My friends were all in the top reading group. This was just one instance where I felt that I was "less than." My gram did model what it looked like to have a love of reading. She especially loved poetry and shared so many of her favorites with me. Her most favorite was "Trees" by Joyce Kilmer.

It took time for me to catch up, and, like her, I learned to have a true appreciation and love for reading, books and poetry.

11

When I received ice skates as a Christmas gift when I was young, she let me put them on and walk on the linoleum in the kitchen to try to get used to them. She didn't mind the marks and divots they left. Our house had old steam radiators that were gray. In the winter months, I loved to spend time outside playing in the snow. Nothing matched the excitement of listening to the radio early in the morning to hear if school was canceled. On those days, nothing made me happier than to be able to build a snowman in front of our sunroom window. When I would come back inside, she'd put my hat and mittens on top of the radiator to dry. I can still remember the hissing sound those radiators made when the heat kicked up.

She would always wear a special decorative pin on the left side of her afternoon dress, and I would be in awe as I watched her add a little red rouge to her cheeks. The rouge was in a small, round gold pot that she kept on her vanity. A bottle of Shalimar perfume was next to the fancy hairbrush and comb set that was gold-rimmed and had a light floral pattern on the back. More than once I tried to add color to my cheeks from this magical pot that I was awed by. But I ended up looking like my cheeks were on fire. My aunt often gave her a bottle of Oil of Olay moisturizer, and she'd say, "I like that Olay, it gives me color." In the 17 years with her, she never wore pants. In fact, never—not once in her life.

I loved to hear stories of her childhood and family, plus Irish traditions that continued into each generation. When a family member passed away, they were laid out in the living room for the viewing, not a funeral home. People took turns staying up all night with the body, so the deceased would not be alone. I had a hard time visualizing that a casket would be where her chair now was. When my grandfather was courting her, they went for rides in the horse and buggy. It sounded so romantic.

She had lost her mother to meningitis when she was only

12, and her grandmother was an integral part of *her* life. My grandfather passed away when she was only 59. She had lived alone until I moved in and became her focus. I was often told that having me with her was what kept her going. One day while visiting her in the nursing home not long before she passed, she said, "I had three children, but you and I are different." The memory of seeing the love in her beautiful green eyes fills my heart to this day.

When I was growing up, she'd play Scrabble with me, and I loved it on Sunday after-noons when she got the card table out so we could play double solitaire. I so treasured our time together.

The front porch of the house was where she often shared so much about her life. I sat on one of the porch chairs, as she sat on the black wrought iron glider. The six cush-ions had one pattern on the front, a different one on the back. She favored the side up with the orange abstract design on it. With her right leg crossed over her left, she gently moved her left leg to create a rhythmic rocking back and forth—an easy tempo that remained consistent until she stopped to get up and go back into the house. She always wore her cream-colored, synthetic fiber sweater draped over her shoulders, with the top button hooked. Her favorite time to sit out on the porch was when it was raining. I clearly remember the sound of the raining spilling from the eves and hitting the spot on the ground just behind the huge trees. When loud claps of thunder erupted, she'd say, "The angels are bowling." I would immediately envision humongous angels with long flowing hair, white robes, and gigantic wings.

My gram never learned to drive. Thankfully, we lived in an area in town where you could walk to most everything. She had a couple of friends who were able to drive her places when needed. Each of these women had their own unique personalities and were so sweet. One of her friends, that really stood out to me, was Marie. Her perfectly coiffed, pure-white hair was always meticulously styled. The deep red lipstick she wore left such an impression on me. I thought it was stunning, such a contrast to her porcelain skin. Always fashionably dressed, with outfits completed by a hat and elbow-length white gloves. She carried herself very gracefully and her posture was perfect. Her perfume lingered in our house long after she came to visit. Her home was full of gorgeous antiques. I'd never seen anything like it—very Victorian. I believe that's when my love and appreciation of anything Victorian began. Though I was young, I recognized that this was a woman of style and sophistication. I think on some level, I imagined that this would be what my mom resembled if she had lived to be in her 70s.

Gram's friend, Mrs. Doherty, picked us up each Sunday for 8 a.m. mass. Around 7:40 a.m., the phone would ring, and on the other line it was always the same thing, "I'll be down in about five minutes." Mrs. Doherty was a very petite woman. I often wondered how her feet reached the gas pedal and brakes. She drove this little yellow car whose interior always smelled like stale flowers. She was always so positive and upbeat.

My gram's Catholic faith was incredibly important to her. As much as I always wanted to sleep in on Sunday mornings, off we went. Females were expected to cover their heads with a mantilla when attending mass. I can best describe that it looked like a white doily. I remember when she forgot to bring it with us, she literally took a bobby pin and attached a Kleenex to the top of my hair. I would look around during the priest's long homily to the families that were there together. Mother, father, children—all together—in what I imagined was a perfect family. I couldn't comprehend what it felt like to have that.

We never ate breakfast before we went, since we were supposed to have the Eucharist on an empty stomach. The majority of the mass was in Latin; I was bored and clueless. I wanted to get home and eat breakfast. Food was my comfort.

I was, however, mesmerized by the huge marble altar and the enormous light fixtures suspended from the high ceiling. I was captivated when during special masses, the priest would walk down the center aisle holding the thurible of burning incense. It made a clanking sound as the metal censer knocked against the chain he was holding. I loved the smell of the frankincense!

She made sure I attended catechism classes. I would often ask questions about certain topics and I was always told the same thing, "It's a mystery."

It's funny how certain memories remain with you. I would have moments when I wanted to talk to my gram about how I was feeling about the loss of my mom. Hers was a generation where painful experiences were not talked about. I knew she had lost her own mother when she was 12, but never did she talk about it. On Mother's Day when I was about 11, she was in the kitchen making chicken. I told her I didn't want to eat because I was missing my mom. Her reaction was not something I was prepared for. She slammed the pot down and as her voice was cracking, she said, "There's a hole in *my* heart, too!" It shocked me. At the age I was, I had no comprehension of how this gut-wrenching loss stays with you your whole life.

Until I was older, I didn't have the true appreciation of just how incredible she was. I'm now 60, and when I feel tired, I stop and reflect on her willingness and energy to start a whole new chapter of her life: raising a 5-year-old at age 72.

My friends and their families were so good to me growing up. Despite having this, I always felt different, like I didn't fit in, that I was never enough. I even went through a period of time where I thought I was adopted. My low self-esteem and self-loathing constantly told me that I wasn't smart enough, pretty enough, thin enough—whatever it was, I wasn't enough. I continually turned to food as a way to not feel anything. My grandmother made lots of homemade cookies, mostly chocolate chip, and having just one cookie never satisfied me. At Christmas time she made her famous lebkuchen cookies. These were most like a soft gingerbread cookie, made with molasses and full of warm spices.

At times her statements were so confusing. "You have such a pretty face, it's a shame you are so fat, here, have a cookie." It confirmed my feeling of being worthless. I wanted to be like my friends. I didn't want to be me.

For about a two-year period, my gram rented out one of the spare bedrooms. Each of the tenants were extremely sweet, and I remember they were very kind and respectful to my gram. We had one phone in the sunroom downstairs and the other one was upstairs in her bedroom. The one in the sunroom was beige and the one in her bedroom was black. Each was a rotary phone with a short cord, so you needed to either sit down or stand right where the phone was to have a conversation—no freedom to walk around. They were able to use either phone.

She had an air conditioner unit in her bedroom window that faced Church Street. About 5 p.m. on the hot balmy summer nights, she would turn it on and close the door so by 10, her routine bedtime, the room was nice and cool and delightful to sleep in. Her bedroom held her full-size mahogany antique bed and a day bed that was in the far corner up against the wall. It was covered by a three-sided harvest gold corduroy cover, and three matching oversized loose pillows that were always smooshed up against the wall. My mom's cucumber green Singer sewing machine was on a table right next to the daybed. I loved that it was displayed. I loved anything tangible that was once hers. On those incredibly hot nights, I slept in that daybed and loved it. More than anything, I felt so safe in the same room with her.

As I would take my bath before bed, she would often lay my clean nightgown on her bed for me to put on before I went to bed. One night, I walked naked from the bathroom into her room to get my nightgown. The door was closed and I could hear the air conditioner running. I opened the door and the man who was renting a room was standing there talking on the phone. He didn't even pay attention to my entering the room. I, however, started screaming and ran back to the bathroom and slammed the door. My gram was trying to get me to open the door. I literally was crying and trembling. I had a flashback...a frightening one.

Before my mother's passing and moving to Pennsylvania, my friend Kathy and I were playing in front of the apartment building we lived in. We looked up, and there was a man behind the front door, looking at us from the glass section at the top of the main entrance. He motioned to us. As he opened the door, he said, "Do you girls want to see Peter Pan?"

The classic *Peter Pan* movie starring Mary Martin had been rebroadcast on TV not long before. Kathy and I were both mesmerized by its magic. Her favorite was Tinkerbell, while I was so taken with Peter Pan... to be able to fly! That's what I wanted!

Of course, we wanted to see Peter Pan.

As you entered the front door to the building, you went down about 10 steps. The apartment I lived in was just on the left. Straight across from our apartment was the laundry room. He led the way, with Kathy and I behind him. Neither one of us felt afraid; this man was offering to show us something magical.

He was wearing a long trench coat, glasses and a hat. For whatever reason, I stopped at the doorway entrance, but Kathy followed him. I heard him say, "This is Peter Pan." I looked and saw him unzip his pants and pull out something. It was his penis. I yelled at the top of my lungs and ran to my apartment door, pounding on it for someone to let me in. I screamed to my parents telling them what just happened.

My dad went flying out the door to catch him, but he was gone. I remember a policeman showed up and I was asked to describe in detail what had happened. The face of that predator remained in my memory.

When I entered my gram's bedroom that night for my nightgown, the awfully nice border on the phone suddenly became the man who exposed himself. It shook me. I didn't feel safe. Eating chocolate-filled cookies helped me not to think about it.

There was a wooden, white-painted swinging door that separated our kitchen from the dining room. Gram usually had it pushed up against the refrigerator so the space between the two rooms was open. One Saturday afternoon, the door was closed, and I heard my gram and aunt speaking quietly in the kitchen. I heard my gram say to my aunt, "I'm worried about Gigi; she is so afraid of men. The only man she will be around is her father." I never let on that I heard them.

I remember one Friday spring night, when I was just 14, my gram and I were sitting on the front porch. As we were sitting there talking, a man pulled up in front of the house in a brand new 1973 Ford LTD. It was a unique color, almost a cross between maroon and pink, and it had the longest hood of any car I had ever seen. My dad knew this man. His name was Gerry. Well known in the community, he was a wealthy, prominent businessman who knew everyone. He and my dad were not friends, merely acquaintances. I loved it when people would say, "You're John Kilroe's daughter!" Yes, I was and very proud to be.

Gerry rolled down the window and motioned for me to get in. "Let me take you for a ride in my new car!" I felt no fear; he knew my Dad, so I didn't think twice. My Gram was not happy, but I simply said "I'll be right back!"

Gerry was in his late 50s or early 60s. Short and stocky with tons of silver hair and a bushy mustache. Dressed in 1970s fashion, he wore white polyester pants, a shirt with a loud print that had a huge, splayed collar that was opened to show masses of chest hair and his gold chains. He was always chewing gum, and the cologne he wore I can best describe as invasive and harsh. He and his then girlfriend owned and operated a card store on Main Street for a short time. At that point in time, I absolutely loved the drawings by Betsey Clark, which were described as "Wide Eyed Waifs." I use to call them the "Onion Heads." In his store, they carried lots of Betsey Clark merchandise. I was saving my money to buy the scrapbook. On the front it read, "Happy Memories Are to Treasure." Two of the little wide-eyed waifs were on the front, and pastel colored patchwork designs made up the boarders. Oh how I wanted that scrapbook. Every time I went into the store to see if the scrapbook was still there, Gerry was always very friendly. I figured he was so nice because of my dad.

I was shocked and confused when things turned dark once I was in the car.

I don't think we were even two blocks up the street when he reached over and put his right hand on my left thigh. I felt myself freeze. I slowly moved my leg away and he finally released his grip. I literally was frozen in fear. He began to laugh.

Just then a woman was riding towards us on her bicycle. He rolled down the window and with his tongue started making large licking movements and noises at her. Then he turned to me and said, "She's a lezzy... you know what they do? They LICK each other!" I didn't understand what he was talking about. All I knew was that I was beyond frightened. I was terrified. He continued to laugh, then asked me, "So, what do you like to drink?" I calmly said, "Please take me home. My grandmother will wonder where I am." I could feel myself sweat from feelings of panic and terror. Thankfully he did take me home, and I couldn't get out of that car fast enough.

I didn't say anything to my gram. I didn't want her to worry, so I swallowed my feelings. The next morning, the phone rang—that beige rotary phone in the sunroom. Long before caller ID, we never knew who was on the other line. I answered it. It was Gerry.

He had an apartment right around the corner from where we lived. He actually said, "So, would you like to come over and have a drink?" The fear came back. I remember I could feel my face turn red and I started to sweat. I wasn't able to express that he made me want to vomit. I simply said, "No" and then hung up.

There I was, a naïve and trusting 14-year-old girl. He knew my dad, so I never thought his motive would be anything other than being friendly. Growing up we learned of "stranger danger." The predator was the man that would chase you down the alley late at night. Never, ever was it mentioned that children were more likely to be harmed by someone they knew.

This wealthy, prominent well-known businessman was a predator. I was clueless to think that a man, almost 60 years old, would have a proclivity for young girls. Predators don't just target one. I shudder to think of how many other young girls in our hometown were preyed upon by his evilness.

That experience left me feeling dirty and full of shame. At that time, I thought it was my fault. I must have done something to make him think that was okay. I never told my dad, but I wish I had. One punch from Big John would have taken care of him.

Today, I picture that scene having a different ending. I visualize myself getting ready to get out of the car, but first I lean over and punch him in the balls as hard as I can—so hard that he screams in pain. Take that, Gerry, you sick bastard.

I did finally save up enough money to buy that scrapbook. I went into that card store for the last time to buy it, and how interesting, he totally ignored me. In fact, any other time after that if I saw him, he completely ignored me. Every time I saw him, I felt dirty and nauseous.

In high school, I started dating a young man who was

handsome, intelligent, from a prominent family and who, in time, became an abuser. It didn't start out that way. It never does. When we had the slightest disagreement, he flew into a rage. My grandmother really liked him. He was so charming with her. Though she saw the bruises, she wanted me to stay with him. She knew he and I were not sexually involved and I truly believe she was more worried about me getting pregnant. I certainly understand that, in the era when she grew up, that was a horrible shame to the family. Sadly, as a result of her not addressing the bruises, the message seemed to be that I just needed to put up with it. My feelings of safety and self-worth were critically damaged.

> "Extremely toxic people will only be abusive
> with a select few; this way their behavior
> won't be found out by the majority."
> – Tamara Yancosky

I never told a teacher; only my closest friends knew. At that point in my life, I believed I deserved his cruelty and abuse. He would say things like, "You are so fat, ugly, and stupid. You might as well stay with me; you'll never amount to anything. No one else would want you." I believed it. He called me "Moosie" and constantly made fun of my large breasts. My breasts became the greatest focus of his cruelty. He punched my breasts—very hard—as wells as my arms. He would kick me in the shins, punch me in the small of the back, pinch me until that area nearly went numb and bend my fingers back, all while yelling, "Tell me you love me!" There are still three scars on my left hand between my thumb and wrist from where he dug his fingernails into me. I was by no means morbidly obese, but I allowed his judgment of my body to permeate and scar my already delicate psyche. It was a grueling relearning through the years of how to release those "old tapes" that played in my head.

In our high school physical education class, the girls

were required to participate in group showers after class before changing back into our clothes. My breasts would have purple and green bruises covering them. I endured the horror of classmates pointing and laughing, thinking they were hickeys. At age 15, I thought I'd end up with breast cancer from all the punching. No 15-year-old adolescent should carry that thought. One afternoon, we were driving back from a movie. He suddenly pulled up to the gate of the hospital for the criminally insane and told me he was having me committed. He laughed maniacally and I literally trembled with fear at the dark evilness in his eyes. I remember the sheer panic I felt.

Being in a relationship with an abuser is very complicated. There were times when he could truly be fun to be with. He was so bright and had a good sense of humor. I remember thinking that he meant it each time when he said he would never hit me or berate me again. But the truth is, it did happen again, and again, and again.

I was a teenage girl who didn't have the strength nor the wherewithal to know how to get out. I didn't know how a young woman deserved to be treated in a relationship. I needed my grandmother's support, but it wasn't there.

> "The toxic monster you saw in the end
> is who they really are, never doubt yourself again
> when they act nice."
>
> – E.S.

I look at photos of myself during that time period. I tried so hard to look like anyone other than me. I had long, naturally curly hair that I tried to straighten because I hated it. Then, I had my hair cut short and I hated it even more. I wore glasses and braces until the middle of my senior year of high school. The braces came off and I got my first pair of contact lenses. I thought those two things would make me happy. No, I still had such self-hatred. I was a very long way from the truth, that learning to love yourself begins with a journey inward.

Those high school years contained so much pain for me. It felt like I could not get away from him. We had classes together and hung out with the same friends. I could not wait for graduation, so I could finally be free.

He took my high school class ring our senior year and would not return it until we graduated. I loved that ring. It was white gold with a beautiful aquamarine stone. Though it wasn't my birthstone, that gorgeous shade of blue has always been one of my favorites. He had control over almost every area of my life. I never knew what would set him off. It was like being in a constant state of hypervigilance and it was exhausting. The scars on my left hand where he dug his fingernails into me will forever be a reminder of what I survived.

> *"It's easier to penalize me for my reaction to your behavior than it is for you to own that you elicited that response by how you treated me."*
> *– Bishop T.D. Jakes*

At the time, I had no awareness that I did not deserve to be treated with such cruelty and abuse. Because of my low self-esteem and the passive reaction from my grandmother to what was happening, I was the perfect, vulnerable target. A few nice young men were interested in dating me. Yet she made me feel I needed to stay exactly where I was. She would say, "But I don't worry when you are with him." That was validation at that time that I needed to accept the abusive situation I was in, apparently I didn't deserve anything better. Talk about confusion. What she saw was a handsome young man who was from a prominent, Catholic family. He could turn on the charm with her. But what I endured, being on the receiving end of his anger and rage, is not something any young woman should have to experience.

I actually wrote a letter to "Dear Abby" my senior year. I poured my heart out and I did receive a letter back. The main message was that I was a strong young woman. Whatever inner demons plagued him were not an excuse for him to unleash his fury onto me. Years later, he did apologize but the residuals left from that experience were not so easy to dismiss.

It would be years and years from that time period before I would know my worth, strength and beauty.

This is the only area that I feel my gram let me down. In every other aspect she was an incredibly wonderfully strong, kind, generous, gracious and independent woman who taught me a great deal.

A Taste of Freedom

The summer after high school graduation, I took a job at a month-long day camp for students with special needs. I was headed to college in August but wasn't sure what I wanted to study.

Somewhere around the second day, this little camper, whose name was Jimmy, walked right up to me. He took me by the hand, looked me dead in the eyes and said, "I like you!" This is what I refer to as my aha moment. I knew at that exact second, working with students with special needs was exactly what I wanted to do. That precious little guy had no idea he changed my life.

College life began in the late 1970s—my first taste of freedom—and I loved it.

My gram was quite strict with my curfew but now I didn't have one. The very first weekend, I went to a party and proceeded to drink 20 Styrofoam cups of beer in 20 minutes. Whatever party you went to, it was a $2 cover and you could drink as much as you wanted. Ah, the stupidity of youth. So, stumbling back to my room in the dorm, I proceeded down the hall and threw up in front of about four rooms. It's amazing the girls on my floor ever spoke to me again. It became a joke as we all got to know one another. "Oh, you are the one that puked in front of my room!" Ah yes, that would be me.

In those days, there was a phone in each room. We would wait to call family after a certain hour when it would be cheaper. No computers then, but I was a proud owner of a manual typewriter. Yes, always the procrastinator, I was the one in the study lounge typing the paper at 4 a.m. that was due for my 8 a.m. class. If you made a mistake while typing, there were two options—the little slips of correction tape or the correction fluid. I preferred the fluid, though I always made a mess and that damn bottle seemed to dry out quickly.

My friend, Stacey, was also a night owl. We would ride the elevators at 2 a.m. eating peanut butter TastyKakes, drinking Tab and laughing hysterically. That Tab was just nasty, but we figured it canceled out the calories of the TastyKakes. I would do anything to avoid studying. I was much more focused on the social aspect of college and decorating my dorm room.

My orange milk crates were stacked on my desk in the dorm room. My hot rollers, photos and books were all there. A handsome male model was featured in magazines for Windsong perfume. "I can't seem to forget you. Your Windsong stays on my mind," was the slogan. My goal was to cover as much of our wall space with his photo. I can't tell you how many magazines I bought just for that photo.

I still to this day love the music from the '70s. When I hear Billy Joel's "The Stranger," Fleetwood Mac's "Rumors," Foghat's "Fool for the City" and Boston's "Boston," those albums make me smile and think of my time in college. I loved walking down the hall in the dorm and hearing music coming from different dorm rooms. But yes, my all-time favorite was disco and funk. The Gap Band, Parliament, Prince, Earth Wind & Fire and Chaka Kahn are all artists I continue to listen to today. On the weekends, I'd travel to my favorite places to dance, in my wraparound Danskin skirt and bodysuit, and yes... those platform heels. When the movie *Saturday Night Fever* was released, we loved it!

> *"I love hearing old songs I used to love.*
> *They are like memories you can always go back to."*
> *– www.theteenagerquotes.tumblr.com*

All you have to do is Google "Fashion from the '70s" to see what now looks a bit ridiculous, but we loved it.

It was so wonderful to make friends with a variety of people. Many became lifelong friends. It was amazing to be surrounded by men and women of similar interests.

Before my sophomore year, I had dropped about 30 pounds and my hair had grown out. The haircut named "The Savage," that I did *not* rock freshman year, was probably one of the worst ideas I ever had. What looked great on the hairstylist did not translate as great on me. I was never satisfied with what I looked like. I always wanted to emulate someone else.

Funny how even though I was in my best shape physically and was getting a lot of attention from guys, I was still plagued with insecurities and self-hatred. I never, *ever* felt I was good enough. Despite looking better physically, how I felt about myself on the inside had not changed. Those old tapes of constantly feeling unworthy continued to play in my head.

When I was a sophomore in college, my roommate set me up on a blind date with a guy from one of her classes, Mick. We both were not dating anyone at the time, and since she knew we both loved different kinds of music, she thought we would click. I remember it happened to be a weekend in October when most students were gone. I was 18 years old, extremely trusting and quite naive. He suggested going to his room in the fraternity house so I could see his album collection. I thought nothing of it.

He starts making drinks that were incredibly strong... I can still smell the gin. Before I know it, he is on top of me—ripping at my clothes. I am crying and yelling, "No," which falls on deaf ears.

He raped me. He was brutally forceful; the physical pain was horrendous. During the rape, he called me Leslie, his ex-girlfriend's name.

Walking back to my dorm room was a blur. I could not process what just happened; I was a virgin until this night. When I got back to the dorm, I went into the bathroom and my underwear was filled with blood. Being naïve, I thought my period had started, and I attempted to use a tampon. The pain was excruciating. I knew something was wrong and I was filled with fear and panic. I didn't know what to do. I was afraid to call my now 85-year-old grandmother. I was afraid if I called my dad he would drive there and kill him. So, I called a childhood friend who was a nursing student at a hospital about 10 miles from the college. I was so grateful she answered the phone. I drove there and she went to the ER with me. Again, this is the '70s—there were no rape kits. Law enforcement wasn't called. All I know is I felt like this was my fault.

Never ever underestimate how important acts of kindness are. The nurse in the room with us was wonderful. The first doctor that came in had not an ounce of kindness or empathy. The first thing he said to me was "Where are you in your cycle?" I said, "About day 14," to which he replied, "Well, you are probably pregnant." I burst into tears and started shaking. Then I saw the nurse put her hand on his back and slowly walk him out of the room. A few minutes later, she returned with a different doctor, who I have to say was amazingly kind and gentle.

Upon examination, he found I had a tear in my vaginal wall an inch-and-a-half long. He told me he was going to have to give me stitches. The pain of that Novocain needle felt like I was being raped all over again. My poor friend, Jill, stayed with me during this ordeal. I squeezed her hand so hard, I'm surprised I didn't break it. After the doctor sewed me up, he packed me with the longest piece of gauze I had ever seen. I was so dazed and stunned that when we first arrived at the ER, I could not even say the words, "I was raped." Instead, I said, "I had intercourse for the first time and something is wrong." I remember the nurse's words, "I don't know who this guy is, but I don't like him very much. The day will come when you will share this with your daughter." Little did I know that forty-plus years later, I'd turn this tragedy into empowerment. Honestly, her words were validation to me that maybe this wasn't my fault. The kindness that she and Jill showed me that night was beyond a blessing and was never forgotten.

I never went to any authorities; only my closest friends knew. I felt like it was my fault. I should not have been alone in his room with him. I should not have been drinking. The next day he called my dorm room and said, "Whatever you do, don't tell anyone I raped you." I threw the phone. It just dangled there as I crawled on top of my bed and started sobbing.

For a week, I stayed in bed and skipped my classes. I had to return to the hospital in 10 days, so the gauze packing could be removed. Shame was the feeling that would not leave me. Intense feelings of embarrassment and numbness remained. I felt damaged, violated and worthless. No one knew to suggest that I go see a counselor. Times were so different then. There was no women's center on campus. I never thought to go to the police because I thought I brought it all on myself. With the evidence from the hospital procedure, I undoubtedly could have had him arrested and thrown out of school. But I wasn't strong enough to do anything about it. I was a scared, naïve, 18-year-old. I truly understand why so many victims keep their silence. In no way could I have handled being cross-examined in court. I had seen too many movies and television shows where they made the victim look like she asked for it.

I did the best I could at the time, I buried it. Life went on. But in time, years later, I learned nothing stays buried forever.

He was a junior, so I would occasionally see him on campus. Every time I saw him, I felt such fear and anxiety. I was so glad when he graduated and left.

Because my personal boundaries had been obliterated, I developed some rather risky behaviors. I desperately wanted love, but instead had sex. It became somewhat of a game to me, setting my sights on someone at a party or a bar and making it my mission to seduce them. It gave me a false sense of power. The encounters were neither sexually nor emotionally satisfying for me. My distorted thinking at the time was, "Well, maybe the next one will be." So young, and so damaged, I had no idea how much, or what, I needed to heal.

I compartmentalized the rape and tucked it away. But one night, at the end of my sophomore year, I experienced my first flashback of the rape.

My roommate and I went to see the movie, *Looking for Mr. Goodbar*. I had no idea what the plot was. At the very end of the movie when Diane Keaton's character is raped and murdered, I immediately flashed back to being raped in the fraternity house. I started trembling and sobbing. I buried my head in my roommate's shoulder. After that experience, I buried everything even deeper. I wasn't able to deal with it, so if I could make sure it stayed buried, I'd be okay, or so I thought.

In spite of the bad memories, the fun times of those four years have given me other memories—good memories, ones I cherish and cling to. Many of the friends I made have remained in touch with each other. We laugh hysterically reminiscing about all the fun and adventures we had.

Unlike having an iPhone today, we had little cameras with those blue flash cubes. You could get four flashes on each cube. Once the flash was used, it automatically turned so you would be ready for the next photo. You had to send the film away and patiently wait for the finished photos to be sent back to you. The suspense... I treasure the few photos I have from those days.

My dad let me have his 1968 Chrysler Newport convertible. It was gold with a black top and black interior. It was huge, like driving your dining room down the street. He used to say, "It'll pass anything, except a gas station." The dimmer switch was on the floor. It had air conditioning and an AM/ FM radio. I thought it was the coolest ever.

I have such incredibly fun memories of adventures in that car. I called it Jonathan, and a friend of mine nicknamed it, "The Whale." Driving down the road with the top down, trying to dodge the raindrops... windshield wipers on, heat blasting, AM radio blaring and eight of my closest friends piled in with me. We headed off on an adventure, laughing hysterically. Priceless.

The first semester of my senior year, I lived in a house with 16 other girls called The Red House. I don't think you could ever find 16 more different women, but we had a blast and it worked. Susie, my friend from high school, was going to be my roommate, so we traveled down the summer before senior year so she could see it. Now, I had lived there for six weeks earlier that summer because I took two classes: child psychology and bowling. (My dad wanted to know why I got a "C" in child psychology but an "A" in Bowling. Umm...good question, Dad.)

I knew on the trip down, that I didn't have a key, and that one of us would have to climb through the window above the front door, and it wasn't going to be me. Yes, I hoisted her up on my shoulders, and she was able to crawl through the window, drop down, and let us in. We laugh about it to this day—the fact was I didn't lie to her. I just didn't tell her everything.

It was a huge house with the most bizarre colors inside, which I'm assuming was because the owner had gotten the paint on sale.

The bathroom was painted black. The furniture was pretty nasty, and then there was the couch...THE couch. I recall the ugliest combination of brown and harvest gold, in a pattern that would want to make you hurl your lunch.

In Susie's and my room the walls alternated between "screaming violet" and "bottom of the swimming pool green."

I had outgrown my love for the Windsong Man, and had moved on to Kris Kristofferson. In 1978 Kristofferson had come out with the album, "Easter Island." While walking by the record store in town, I spotted the humongous poster of the album cover in the window.

I'm not a fan of country music, but I wanted that poster. Kristofferson's salt and pepper beard and crystal clear blue eyes were intoxicating. He was wearing a white shirt with the neck open, and there was a blue sky and clouds in the background. The blue of the sky brought out that incredible luscious blue in his eyes.

I went into the store and talked the owner into giving me the poster. I may have done a little sweet-talking and flirting. Once in my possession, I hung it up in Susie's and my room. It was a great distraction from the absurd color combo on the walls.

To this day, she remembers the day she said, "Gig, aren't you going to your 3 p.m. class?" Apparently, my answer was, "I can't go to class; I don't have a pen." *General Hospital* was on at 3 p.m. and I was among countless loyal fans who were waiting for Luke and Laura to get together… priorities.

The universe has a sense of humor. Years later, I ended up teaching three different classes as an adjunct instructor at this university. The very first class I would tell them how they needed to be at every class—that I knew all the excuses—and smirked as I gave each of them a brand-new pen.

The second semester of my senior year was student teaching. I moved in with my dad and stepmother in south Jersey since the school I was assigned to was outside of Philadelphia, and only about 25 minutes from their home.

My stepmother had five good years after her breast cancer, but it came back in her lungs. My dad was now facing losing his second wife to cancer. It just hurt my heart to see him have to go through losing her.

"What Cancer Cannot Do
Cancer is so limited...
It cannot cripple love
It cannot shatter hope
It cannot corrode faith
It cannot destroy peace
It cannot kill friendship
It cannot suppress memories
It cannot silence courage
It cannot invade the soul
It cannot steal eternal life
It cannot conquer the spirit."

— Author Unknown

One day, when I came home from student teaching, she was in bed with oxygen tubes going from her nostrils to the tank. I flashed back to seeing my mom. I bolted to my room and just sobbed. I suddenly became that 5-year-old child again. That "hole in my heart," as my gram phrased it, was very much there.

On weekends, I traveled back to see my gram or to see my friends at college.

After graduation, I moved back home with my gram. She was slowly starting to decline. My friends started their new lives in different cities and I now became my gram's caregiver. I never regretted one moment and would do it all again.

It was time to be a responsible adult.

"She lost herself in the trees among the
ever-changing leaves. She wept beneath
the wild sky as stars told stories of ancient times.
The flowers grew towards her light, the river
called her name at night. She could not live an
ordinary life with the mysteries of the
universe hidden in her eyes."

— Christy Ann Martine

Different Shades of Trauma

$\mathcal{I}$ was hired as a first-grade teacher 65 miles from my gram's house. It was a one-year assignment covering for someone's maternity leave. The days were long and I always worried each morning when I left her. While I was growing up, there were nights that I would stand just outside her bedroom, listening for her breathing. I'd hear her take a deep breath, then exhale. I felt the paralyzing fear that each exhale was her last. I felt such trepidation that she would die in her sleep and I would be left alone. After I would listen for a while, I tiptoed back to my room. I never shared this fear with anyone. The feelings of anxiety and dread were suffocating. I hadn't truly grieved my mom's death, and now the mother figure who nurtured me and loved me would also be leaving. I knew it was inevitable.

When my students were at one of their specials, I'd go to the main office and try calling her. But because her hearing was getting worse, she wouldn't always hear the phone. I would be on pins and needles the rest of the day, and so grateful to get home and find she was okay.

I loved my first-grade class, though I certainly had my challenges as a first-year teacher. I learned what to do and what I would do differently in my next position. Their innocence and excitement in learning was pure joy. One day, one of my students said, "I like that mug." I said, "Thank you! My dad gave it to me." He looked at me with a confused look on his little face and said, "You have a dad?" So precious. I promised my students that when they graduated from high school, I would be there—and I was. It was such a joy to see

35

so many of them and to hear what their future plans were.

By March, my gram needed more care than I was able to give. My father, aunt and uncle together made the painful decision that she needed to move to a nursing home. I realized you can start grieving for someone before they are actually gone.

With my gram now settled in the nursing home and our house sold, I moved to New Jersey. It was so painful to leave the home I shared with her. In my heart, it would always be home. The house that held so many warm and loving memories would now become a dental office.

I drove up to see her every other week. Slowly, she weakened. No longer able to walk, she spent most of the time in her wheelchair. There was a huge, open visitation room that resembled a solarium at the end of her hall. The carpet was maroon, as was the upholstery on the couches and chairs. White wainscoting was on the bottom half of the walls, while the maroon flower pattern wallpaper went to the ceiling. Brass electric candle sconces were on each wall. In the center of the room not far from the farthest wall was a piano. As I wheeled her down the hall to that room, we'd pass other residents sitting in the hallway in front of their rooms. I spoke to them all—some smiled—some yelled. One day, I said hello to Wanda, who was three rooms down, when she surprisingly reached up and punched me in the arm. I felt such sadness for the residents and for my gram. My heart sank every time I left the facility through those front automatic doors. I felt guilty that this was now her home and that I was no longer able to care for her. She wasn't ever coming home.

She loved to hear me play the piano. I positioned her wheelchair so she could be right there watching as I played. Those beautiful, sparkling, clear green Irish eyes twinkled as a little smile came over her face when I'd play two of her favorites, "Maple Leaf Rag" and "In the Mood." We weren't together in our home on Church Street, but we were able to spend some time together. Home, I learned, is not always a place, but a feeling. Whenever I was with her, no matter where it was, was home.

I began taking piano lessons in the fourth grade and continued until I graduated from high school. My teacher focused on classical music, which at the time I didn't truly appreciate. My piano teacher and her twin sister gave lessons out of their home. They were graduates from the Eastman School of Music and incredibly talented. Their two pianos were in the center of the room back-to-back. I would be in awe watching them play two-piano duets. I certainly learned a great deal from them. Because I wanted to explore other types of music, I would pick up piano sheet music of different genres and slowly learn songs without her help.

There was, however, one particular classical piece I desperately wanted to learn how to play, "Prelude in C# minor" by Rachmaninoff. I purchased the sheet music and took it to her for help when I was a sophomore in high school. I will never forget when she kind of chuckled and smugly said, "You can't play that!" I think for the very first time in my life, I felt a surge of energy and anger inside me. I thought to myself, "Really? Watch me!"

Always feeling less than, that I wasn't good enough, was not happening with this. I didn't care how long it took me, I was going to master it. I practiced for hours and hours and days and days. On some level, playing this powerful piece of music released emotions deep within me. Days turned into months and I would not give up. I think when she saw how passionate and dedicated I was about this, she started to help me.

I proved her wrong. I did master it. It continues to be one of my favorite pieces of all time. I was asked to play it at our high school chorus concert; I was asked to play it for the women's club. Me? Yes me! For once, I believed in myself.

Perhaps this was my first glimpse into the indescribable feeling that awakens when you follow your true passions.

One of the reasons I decided to move to New Jersey was that my stepmother had just passed away and I wanted to be closer to my dad. I was 22 years old and took a job as the head teacher of 3-year-olds in a preschool center. Not my dream job but I thought the experience would be great. What was challenging for me was the owner of the preschool thought I should be teaching these little 3-year-olds how to read. She wasn't pleased that I was providing activities geared to what was developmentally appropriate for a 3-year-old. It served as a great life lesson on learning how to work with difficult people.

Lenny was a guy who was friends with the owner, who did odd jobs for her. He had a huge crush on another teacher there and would often come to me for advice. One night, he suggested we grab a drink after work; I said sure. He talked about himself the whole time (as some men like to do), state wrestling champ... blah blah blah. Let's talk about me... blah-blah- blah. I'm bored and just want to go home.

My car was parked in front of the preschool. He said he wants me to come in to show me something he is working on. That little voice inside me said "No," but I didn't want to appear rude. Again, I was trusting, naive and, after all, he was a friend of the owner.

As soon as we are inside, he starts making moves. He was not a tall man, but incredibly strong. Before I know it, I was face down on the floor of my classroom. He proceeds to rape and then sodomize me.

I don't remember driving home. I am, again, feeling like it was my fault and I tell no one. I kept thinking no one would believe me. I figured they would say, "Why were you there with him after hours?" Or, "Lenny wouldn't do that! He's such a great guy!" I would now have to go into work every day to the room, my classroom, where I was raped and sodomized.

Event number two... buried, for now.

"It could take you years to actually face what has happened. And numerous more to overcome it."
                                        – Carol Sides

A few months after this assault, I attempted to take my life. I swallowed a bottle of aspirin and drank a bottle of Jack Daniels. It didn't kill me—just made me incredibly sick. I have to say, as soon as I did it, I knew it really wasn't what I wanted. I didn't really want to die. I just wanted the pain to stop and was so clueless as to how to make that happen. I went into the bathroom to try to induce vomiting but all that came up was blood and phlegm. I pulled out my Bible from my bookcase and started reading and praying. I was so afraid to go to sleep that night, fearful I would not wake up.

I did not seek any type of counseling. I dealt with it the best I could at the time, which was pushing it down and staying silent. Just like the rape in college, I feared not being believed. Another layer of shame was now added to my psyche.

I could not continue to go into that building day after day. Though I loved my students, I needed to distance myself from the constant reminder of that night. I thought long and hard about what I did want, and it was that feeling I had while working at the summer camp—that feeling that lit the fire inside me and inspired me. I wanted to work with students with special needs. It was time to put a plan in place to make that happen.

"Passion is energy. Feel the power that comes from focusing on what excites you."
                                        – Oprah Winfrey

Just a couple of months later, my grandmother passed away. I was devastated. The woman who was always there for me was gone. I felt empty and lost. The world looked and felt different to me now. That "hole in my heart" that she so perfectly described, felt like a gaping wound in my own soul.

> *"Grief, I've learned, is really just love.*
> *It's all the love you want to give, but cannot.*
> *All that unspent love gathers up in the corners*
> *of your eyes, the lump in your throat, and in that*
> *hollow part of your chest.*
> *Grief is just love with no place to go."*
> *– Jamie Anderson*

As I walked into the room for her viewing and saw her in the casket, my knees went out from under me. My dad was on my right and my aunt was on my left. They each took an arm to hold me up. The excruciating dagger of pain in my heart was overwhelming.

Each time I went to visit her in the nursing home, I brought her one red rose. My hands shook as I placed a red rose in her casket—my last expression of love for her.

I leaned on friends and their moms, but that would never replace what had left my life. She had been a huge gift to me. In time, I realized her influence would be with me always.

> *"Grandmothers are voices of the past*
> *and role models of the present.*
> *Grandmothers open the doors to the future."*
> *– Helen Ketch*

Moving and Growing

I resigned from the preschool, and for a while, I worked as the assistant manager of a cosmetics studio in the mall. It was a great experience because I have always loved makeup! It also brought me somewhat out of my shell, forcing me to learn how to deal with the public. After a time, I realized even more how much I wanted to work with students with special needs. This job wasn't fulfilling. It had been fun, but it was time to go for what my soul really wanted.

I enrolled in graduate school full-time to earn my master's degree. I was excited to return to the same university where I earned my bachelor's. My graduate assistantship paid for the tuition and I took out a loan to pay for living expenses. I rented a tiny apartment, just down the hill from the campus. In the corner of the small living room was the stove, sink, and refrigerator combo—all one unit! The walls were dark paneling, but I didn't care. I always kept photos of family and friends everywhere.

I loved graduate school. I worked hard but had so much fun. The group of us that were there for assistantships spent great times together. I love the saying, "Life is better when you're laughing." It is so true.

One of my fondest memories was the first student I had the opportunity to work with who was on the autism spectrum. He was the thirteen-year-old adopted son of one of our professors. I'll refer to him as "E." For whatever reason, he really took to me. He didn't like the way "Gigi" sounded, so he called me 7979. ("G" being the 7th letter in the alphabet, "I" being the 9th).

All of us in this class spent time with E and I even babysat a couple of times. One day I took him for ice cream, then showed him my apartment. He was mesmerized by one poster I had on the wall. It was of a woman from the 1920s, sitting on a couch with a black cat on her lap. The large tail of the cat hung down making a curved semi-circle. E was fascinated by anything that had curves.

It was 1984, so there were no answering machines or caller ID. My phone would ring, and this would be the exact conversation every time.

Me: Hello
E: 7979 this is E, how are you doing?
Me: I'm fine, how are you?
E: Are you looking at the picture?
Me: No
E: Why not?
Me: (I literally would turn and look at the poster every time)
E: I like the curve of the tail. I like the curve. Can I have that photo?
Me: No
E: Can I have that photo when you die?
Me: OK
E: When are you going to die?

He was fascinating to work with. He was so gifted in so many areas, but social interactions were such a challenge for him.

My friend Courtney stayed in touch with his family after graduate school. One day he called her and it had been a horrible day for her. She shared their conversation.

Courtney: Hello
E: This is E, how are you doing?
Courtney: Not so good, I was fired from my job today.
E: Is it because you are fat?

She said he is the only person in the world she could have taken that from.

"There needs to be a lot more emphasis on what a child can do instead of what he cannot do."
— Dr. Temple Grandin

He was truly a joy to work with and to learn from.

I worked hard and earned my Masters of Science Degree in Exceptional Persons in a year. I was now ready to take on the world!

Though the pain of the past remained buried inside me, I landed my dream job. I worked with students in grades 1-6 who had learning disabilities and emotional challenges. I was never able to have children of my own, so in a way, these were my babies! I had incredible families to work with and our school faculty felt like family.

I would often tell my students I wanted to get a kitten. I never had a pet and now that I had my own apartment, I was ready for one. One day, one of my students came in and said, "Miss Kilroe, you have to come to my house after school. I have a kitten for you!"

In this tall cardboard box was an adorable, all black, furball that was meowing up a storm. I asked him how did he know which one to get for me? He said, "She was knocking her brothers and sisters over." Okay, a feisty one!

For the first two months, I thought it was a girl and named her Lorena. One day my friend Sue was visiting, and she said, "Uh, Gig, this is not a girl". She proceeded to pick her up, turn her over and say, "These are called balls."

Lorena became Sam. He had a great personality and was a great companion. He grew to be 21 pounds and very long. When he walked, his stomach swayed back and forth. My dad nicknamed him "Two Story Sam." He lived to be just about 18. I was crushed when I had to have him put down.

*"Our teachers come in many forms, and I believe one
of these forms is in the shape of a cat. Just when
we need it most, the perfect kitty appears—at least
perfect for us—to be our teacher and help us heal.
That is the karma of cats: to lead us into our purpose
by teaching us how to love unconditionally."*

— Seane Corn

I wanted my students to learn to embrace their own strengths and their own individuality. I had struggled with reading and math in elementary school, so I understood their frustration. I wanted my classroom to be a nurturing, supportive environment for them to learn and grow. Not only did we focus on academic growth, but also on self-esteem. I wanted them to take pride in who they were as individuals. In our Learning Support Room on Valentine's Day, it was Silly Hat Day, St. Patrick's Day was Silly Tie Day. I had so many pockets of joy during my years with the students! One year, I was honored to be nominated for the local Jaycees' "Young Outstanding Educator Award" by the school district I worked in.

Remember how I said, never underestimate acts of kindness? I had this little guy in my room who was so bright but struggled with severe learning disabilities. One day, I called his home to tell his mom what a great day he was having. She started to cry. I asked her, "What's wrong?" I will never forget her answer. She said, "You are the only teacher who has ever called me to tell me he has done something right."

I have never forgotten that. It made me realize the importance of those random acts of kindness. Something so simple can make a difference in someone's day. People, all people, need to hear something positive.

A couple of years ago this particular student, now a grown man, sent me a friend request on Facebook. He is living in Florida and has a successful career. He earned his bachelor's degree and is currently working on his Masters. What he shared with me brought me to tears. He said he had been asked to speak at the National Learning Disabilities Conference, that he would have the floor for 30 minutes to share how he was able to overcome his challenges, and that he was going to share with the audience that I was the person in his educational experience that believed in him. Huge pocket of joy! I had no idea... I can't express how honored I felt.

As a special education teacher, I wanted my students to love and appreciate themselves from the inside out. A lesson I very much needed to learn.

Things were going well during those years. I loved my job and was dating a very sweet guy whose name was Bob. One Saturday we decided to rent the movie, *The Prince of Tides*. For those of you reading this who may be too young to remember, Blockbuster Video were locations where you would rent a movie on an actual VHS tape. You would be charged an extra $2.00 if you didn't rewind it before returning it.

All I knew about this movie was that it starred Barbra Streisand and Nick Nolte. I liked her music and thought he was hot. In the movie Barbra is a therapist and Nick is her client. In one scene, he experiences a flashback. *In his flashback, I see the sister being assaulted. She is on her stomach. I see her little saddle shoes moving... up... and... down.*

At that exact moment, I went into my own MAJOR FLASHBACK. The first flashback I had at the end of my sophomore year in college was nothing compared to this one. I started shaking, crying and sobbing uncontrollably. The poor guy I was dating had no clue why I was having such a reaction. Everything that I had experienced and had pushed down for years came flying up at breakneck speed. I knew I had to face everything and get to a therapist to help me.

I am so blessed that the first therapist I went to was a great match for me. Her name is Leigh, and I call her my angel. Someone told me that when you begin therapy it gets worse before it gets better. Did I want to believe that? As my friend

Judy says, "a hell to the no!" I knew I had so much to work through, but I was so ready to fight those demons to get to the other side of all the pain. I could not walk the journey of healing alone.

With her help, I slowly began to see my strength and my worth. The increments were truly like baby steps. Two steps forward one step back, but I kept going.

About a year into therapy, I had received a questionnaire in the mail from the university I graduated from. I wrote on the form that I had been a victim of a date rape while a sophomore, and if they ever needed a speaker I'd be happy to do so. I never expected to hear anything, and was shocked when they called me. I now had a chance to share my story at my very first "Take Back the Night" event.

In preparation for speaking that night, I went to our town library (these were the days before Google), to find any information I could on date rape. What I found was beyond an eye-opener.

I had no idea that statistics support that one in four women will be sexually assaulted on our college campuses by the time they graduate. A huge percentage of survivors will develop an eating disorder, depression, and/or anxiety. Some become promiscuous; some avoid sex all together. Sitting there alone in this huge library reading all of this, seeing it all in print, was a validation of the emotions and behaviors I had experienced.

Sharing my story that night, my voice cracked and I shook. Though I struggled to get through it, I got through it. Never underestimate the power of speaking your truth. This was a huge step for me.

One young woman came up to me afterwards, with tears in her eyes, and said it had happened to her and that she had not told anyone. I gave her a big hug and talked to her about getting support. When it happened to me, I didn't hear stories from other survivors. I didn't know this had ever happened to anyone else. In talking to this young woman, I hoped our paths crossing that night would put her on a different trajectory. I pray she has been able to take her power back.

A couple of years later, the college printed an alumni directory, and I bought one. I looked my rapist up and found him. He was living in the Midwest. I made a bold decision--I wanted to confront him. I was so filled with fear and anxiety but I wrote him a letter and sent it. I took a risk because I truly didn't know how he would react. The driving force behind my decision was I WANTED TO TAKE MY POWER BACK. I was proud of myself. Not only had I shared my experience of being a date rape survivor at "Take Back the Night," but I also found my rapist and confronted him. I never heard anything from him, which truly didn't matter. What matters is I had developed that internal strength to speak my truth. At the time, I had no idea where this journey would lead me.

Therapy is not easy but it's so worth it. Each person's healing journey is different. It's a process and you can't rush the process. I needed to grieve and mourn so many things and continue to work on self-love, which was so hard for me. What I will tell you is through all of that work, I still felt like there was something beneath it all that I hadn't gotten to.

A friend suggested that I read *Homecoming* by John Bradshaw. The book focused on ways to heal your inner child and offered different exercises throughout the book. One of the exercises was to write a letter to yourself as a child with your non-dominant hand. It was a rainy Saturday morning when I came across this particular exercise. I had an aqua, flowered journal that I started writing in each day. As I turned to a new page I wrote:

> *Dear Little Gigi,*
> *I'll always be here for you.*

What happened next was something that I never experienced before, nor since. I started crying and couldn't stop. I sobbed and sobbed the entire day. Finally, by about 10:00 p.m. that night, I fell asleep. I had such a pounding headache the next morning.

Luckily, I had a therapy appointment early that week. I shared with Leigh what happened. Much later down the road, she said she knew there was something deeply buried that had not surfaced.

What I can best describe is that I was able to heal different parts, but it would take a catastrophic event down the road before I could put all the pieces together. My therapist helped me walk through the grieving process of each part. Working in therapy is a commitment. I knew I wanted to get away from the pain, but I had no idea what it all entailed. There were time periods so difficult for me, but knowing I had an appointment with her kept me focused.

She believed in me, and I trusted her completely. One of the major things I discovered about myself was that I was a huge people pleaser. Somehow early on, I learned to always put the needs and feelings of others ahead of my own. I didn't know I had the right to say "no," not just in romantic relationships but also in friendships. Even when friends wanted to go somewhere or do something I really didn't want to, I would agree just to appease them. Once I had awakened to the realization of this, it felt amazing to be able to be comfortable maintaining my boundaries. I was slowly learning that I had a voice and my voice mattered.

> *"Setting boundaries is a practice of self-love.*
> *You deserve to preserve your peace of mind.*
> *Remove things and people in your life that*
> *no longer serve your best interest."*
> *– Ash Alves*

I struggled with trust and abandonment issues which affects feelings of intimacy in relationships. The inability to experience intimacy in relationships is a definite residual of these issues. In each relationship, I wasn't even aware that my voice mattered. I would always put the man's wants and needs ahead of my own. You see my thinking was always, "I'll do anything, just don't leave me." It wasn't until much later in therapy that I realized my abandonment issues were so deep. I remained in several relationships far too long. The loss of my mother so very young was so detrimental. It took a long time in therapy to really grieve it and to realize that every time I experienced a loss, it triggered that first deep major loss.

"If you have the ability to love, love yourself first."
– Charles Bukowski

I searched in all different ways outside of myself to fill that inner void. Whether it was food, or spending money, I just wanted something to make me feel good. It would work temporarily; then that void would spring open again. In romantic relationships, I was afraid of truly being vulnerable with my feelings and emotions--afraid that if they knew the real me, they'd leave. I tended to choose men that were unavailable. I understand that now, but at the time those choices continuously reaffirmed what I felt deep down, that I wasn't good enough--that I didn't deserve more. My inner dialogue, those old tapes, just kept repeating. I honestly believe I truly learned something from each relationship I've had. As I have reflected, each man taught me more about myself.

I will say there is one man, Jake, who will always remain deeply buried within my heart. I was nineteen and he was much older. Neither one of us expected to fall in love. From the moment we met, there was an instant connection, an immediate feeling that our souls had known each other forever. When I looked into his eyes, it felt like home. It's hard to really describe it, but if you've had a soul connection you understand. I was so young and naïve that I thought I'd easily find that connection again. I have fallen in love a couple of

49

times since, but nothing comes close to the connection and bond I experienced with him.

"Love is not a feeling. Love is spiritual energy.
Love is pure creative energy at its highest level.
Love expressed in human form actualizes your
divine self."
— Barbara King

When I learned he had passed away, it felt like a dagger piercing my heart. This relationship gave me a glimpse of what unconditional love must feel like. It also set a standard for me that a spiritual connection with a partner is essential and non-negotiable. Though we were not meant to be forever, my relationship with him was a true gift. When I remember his gentle nature, and those soft blue eyes, I remember a profound love that touched my life.

"If your heart hurts a little after letting go of
someone or something, that's okay. It just means
that your feelings were genuine. No one likes
endings. But sometimes we have to put things
that were once good to an end after they turn
toxic to our wellbeing. Not every new beginning
is meant to last forever. Not every person who
walks into your life is meant to stay."
— Najwa Zebian

From Teaching to Administration

While I was teaching, I experienced a painful romantic breakup with a man named Chris. I still did not understand how the loss of my mother truly affected me or why typical grieving took so much longer for me. I dealt with the pain by trying to keep busy.

I did private tutoring after school. I provided homebound instruction for students from two different school districts that were temporarily home for medical reasons. I painted the inside of my apartment. I searched for anything to keep my mind occupied. This time period was necessary, and unknowingly, helped prepare me for my next career opportunity.

I began taking courses for my Special Education Supervisory certification, just for something to do. I honestly was content in the classroom and had no intention of ever pursuing a job in administration. I loved each course and learned so much. However, I learned the most from Jim, the amazing administrator I worked with during the supervisory internship. Not only was he brilliant, but I observed how he treated people. He cared, listened and always made decisions based on what was best for the students. So positive and upbeat, he was loved, admired and respected by everyone.

"You don't inspire your teammates by showing
them how amazing you are. You inspire them
by showing them how amazing they are."
– Robyn Benincasa

If I ever had the opportunity to be in a leadership position, I wanted to emulate those qualities. I joke with him to this day that if he needed wiper blades at 2:00 in the morning, I'd go get them for him. When someone believes in you, it brings out your best. He believed in me, my skills, and I'll forever be grateful for his support and all I learned from him.

After I finished my summer internship, I applied for an open supervisory position. Never in a million years, did I think I would land the job. The old tapes in my head kept playing. "I'll fail. I'm not smart enough to do this. I'll end up fired and homeless." I had zero confidence in myself. Fear and anxiety were both front and center, with countless nights of tossing and turning.

It was not an easy decision to leave the classroom, but I took a risk--a huge one--and so glad I did. Had Chris not broken my heart while I was teaching, I would have never pushed myself to go beyond my comfort zone. At the time I thought he ended it because I wasn't good enough for him. In my mind, the woman he left me for and married had everything I did not. My low self-esteem was connected to those old tapes. At the time, I was unable to see the situation from the perspective of a mature adult. It was my inner pain that reacted, and that had nothing to do with him.

> *"It's not what you are that's holding you back.*
> *It's what you think you are not."*
> *– Anonymous*

During my 23 years as a supervisor, I worked with so many incredible teachers. The vast variety included: teachers of the deaf and hard of hearing, teachers of the visually impaired, speech therapists, educational interpreters, an educational audiologist, school psychologists, ESL providers, emotional support teachers, teachers for students with multiple disabilities and autism, school social workers, remedial support teachers in the non-public schools, teachers of the gifted, physical therapists, and educational support providers in county prisons.

I worked for a regional education agency. Nineteen different school districts contracted with us for specific services. The majority of my staff were itinerant, meaning they traveled between districts providing services. The specific area we covered was four thousand square miles. I drove... a lot. I could tell you where you could find the best coffee and the cleanest restrooms, which I had learned from experience!

When I first accepted this position, the gentleman I was replacing had the best advice for me. He said, "Gi, it's not the students or the paperwork that will give you the most trouble. It will be the personalities of the adults." In whatever your work arena is, there will always be challenging people to work with. I learned to listen, without judgment. Sometimes people just need to vent. I remember well one specific incident that happened during my second year of teaching that certainly drove the point home.

I was all revved up for a day of back-to-back parent-teacher conferences. The very first one blindsided me. The mother came in and basically ripped me. Her son wasn't happy, he wasn't learning anything... etc., etc. Prior to this conference, she had never reached out to me with any concerns. I was more than taken back because her son was truly a joy to work with and in fact, was making great progress. I could not understand it and found it difficult to get through the rest of the conferences. I was truly hurt.

Later that night, she called me at home and was crying. She apologized and shared that late the night before, she had received a phone call from her sister, who had just been diagnosed with terminal cancer. I was the first person she saw after that life-changing phone call and she projected and unleashed her anger onto me. She then said she was pleased with her son's educational programming and again apologized for her misplaced anger.

I certainly learned a great deal from this situation. We truly never know what anyone is dealing with in their personal lives.

I had been so afraid to make this career jump from the classroom to administration. I was so afraid of failure, picturing myself and my cat living in a box in the Walmart parking lot. There were plenty of moments when the feeling of self-doubt was crippling. But because I did take a leap of faith, I was given the opportunity to learn from some incredible teachers and get to know some pretty amazing students.

I also had the opportunity to attend state-wide conferences and even make presentations at a few. Having the opportunity to network with other supervisors across the state was so valuable. Because I took that leap of faith and left the classroom, I had the opportunity to grow so much more professionally.

"You don't have to see the whole staircase,
just take the first step."
– Martin Luther King Jr.

At one point, I had a staff of thirty people, each with their own set of skills and strengths. I wanted to know who they each were as a person. It was so important for me to be a supervisor they could trust and count on. My job was to support them and lead by example. Because I saw what that looked like during my internship with Jim, I now had an amazing opportunity to have an impact.

The head of our organization was Tom, a true leader. Like Jim, he inspired each of us, bringing out our best. He'd often quote Theodore Roosevelt, "They don't care how much you know until they know how much you care."

"The role of a creative leader is not to have all
the ideas; it's to create a culture where everyone
can have ideas and feel that they're valued."
– Ken Robinson

The biggest take away here: don't ever be afraid to take a chance.

The other supervisors I worked with were amazing people, all of whom are now lifelong friends. We supported, trusted and valued each other. All of our personalities just clicked together. Even our staff would comment on the great relationship we had among us. We all worked hard and laughed hard. It doesn't get any better than that.

The following from JoinBlush.com sums it up:

Seven Qualities of Successful Friendships:
They laugh at each other's jokes.
There is no competition.
They value honesty.
They stick up for each other.
They are invested in each other.
They normalize each other's experiences.
They accept each other for who they are.

There were so many pockets of joy during these years, like seeing a second grader present a PowerPoint to his class about his hearing loss or watching a visually impaired third-grader demonstrate to her class how she is learning Braille (all while explaining her eye condition and its implications) and attending graduation for a student who was deaf and blind who graduated second in his class. It was so empowering to see my staff working with their students on self-advocacy skills. When I would visit my teachers who worked with students that had emotional issues, I would see a strong emphasis on social and coping skills. For several of the students who had suffered loss and abuse, those coping skills offered tools for them to be able to make more positive choices in their own lives. There I was, a grown adult, thinking to myself, I wish I had had these tools when I was younger. All children need to be taught coping skills. I would think to myself, Why do you need to have a label to be taught these skills? Unless your family models it for you, you find your own way to cope and for me it was always food.

Because I was never satisfied with how I looked, I had a habit of changing not only hairstyles, but hair color. I have been every shade of blonde, brunette and red that you can think of. One time, I went to get a new car and my dad went with me. My father truly had a great sense of humor. We're with the salesman who is filling out the paperwork and he asks me, "Eye color?" I respond, "Hazel." Then he asks, "Hair color?" Before I could open my mouth, my dad says, "Depends what week it is." I still laugh about that.

Because food has been my go-to coping strategy for over 50 years, my weight drastically fluctuated. I had everything from a size 12 to a size 24 in my closets. I've weighed 150 pounds; I've weighed 300 pounds. This has been the biggest residual impact of the abuse. I ask God for guidance and take it one day at a time. I have no doubt that if I had turned to alcohol or drugs, I'd be dead by now. The food addiction eventually took a toll on my body. I developed Type 2 diabetes. The day came when I ended up in the emergency room, thinking I was having a heart attack. My doctor told me if I didn't do something, I'd be dead in five years.

I worked closely with my doctor and my therapist. I would have periods of success regarding my weight. It seemed I could sustain success for about a year-and-a-half, then old habits returned and the number on the scale started to slowly climb. Why, why was this still such a struggle?

> *"The kingdom of heaven is within you,*
> *and whoever shall know himself shall find it."*
> *– Egyptian proverb*

LOSING MY HERO

*a*fter my dad's first stroke, I traveled to see him at his home in New Jersey most weekends. His house was a ranch-style, and he was able to get around, and so prided himself on his independence. Always the proud Irishman. After years of making those trips, I truly wanted him to move to be closer to me. We secured a ground floor apartment in the same complex where I was. For the first time ever, we were both listed in the same phonebook.

Just like his mother, my gram, he enjoyed his routines. His menu for each night of the week remained consistent; Monday night, hot dogs; Tuesday night, pork chops; Wednesday night, hamburger; Thursday night, stew; Friday night, fish; Saturday night, steak; and Sunday was always a roast. Like his mom who put that teaspoon of coffee in her cup each night, he would be sure there was water in the coffee pot so he could turn it on as soon as he woke up. Ironically, both kept a pair of scissors right next to "their" chair. Both were creatures of habit and consistency. I do the same with my own routines. It must be genetic.

I loved having him so close. All the years we lived apart in different areas no longer mattered. What mattered now was this precious time I had with him. The way he could deliver a story was unlike anyone else. Though I had heard them all several times through the years, each time I heard them, I laughed as if it were the first time. I either saw him every day or talked to him on the phone at night. Being a man of routine, the phone call was always at 8 p.m.

I took him to church each Sunday for the 11:15 a.m. mass.

Like my gram, his Catholic faith was extremely important to him. Afterward, we would always go for a long ride and typically go out for lunch.

There was never a loss for words between us. We could talk about anything and everything. He was so easy to be with. His positive outlook and sense of humor were both just wonderful. I treasure each and every photo I have of him and those of us together.

> "Dad,
> You taught me that a bird
> must leave the nest and fly...
> That in time, I would leave
> and soar towards the sky.
> It was your love and guidance
> that reinforced my wings...
> You lifted me before I soared
> towards life's greatest things."
> – Patricia Hacker-Harber

There are many photos that tug at my heart, but especially one in particular. It was a summer day and we were outside. I'm probably about 18-months-old. From photos that I have, it's easy to see my mom always had me in little dresses. My dad told me she dressed me up like her little doll every day, sometimes changing my hair and outfits two to three times. On this particular day, I wore a little dress with a flouncy skirt, little white ankle socks and little white shoes. My left hand is holding onto a couple of fingers on his right hand and I'm standing with my left foot on my right shin. I look so tiny next to this gentle giant. Whenever I held his hand, I felt safe. Whenever I was with him I felt safe. That feeling of his love and protection was with me always, even as an adult.

About five years after the move to be where I was, he started to decline physically. His mind was as sharp as a tack, but when it was discovered that his carotid artery was 100% blocked, his time left was brief. My heart was beyond broken.

I was having to face losing the person I loved more than anyone in the world, my hero.

For years I had asked God to allow me to be with him when he passed and He answered my prayers. All my life, he said if he had to go to a nursing home, he would last two weeks. He lasted 21 days. I spent as much time with him there as I could. The nursing staff was so sweet and kind to me. Each night when I left, I wasn't all the way out the door before I'd burst into tears. The nursing home was on a hill overlooking the city. After getting in my car, I'd stare at all the lights below and wondered how I was going to get through this. The ache in my heart was almost debilitating.

I turned to my drug of choice: food. The pounds just keep piling on. It was my coping mechanism, but it also brought shame, self-hatred and feelings of worthlessness. I felt like a failure. It would be sometime down the road before I would again attempt to conquer this addiction head on.

Less than a week before he passed, I was sitting in the chair next to his bed. I would just watch him sleep, fearing each breath would be his last. I'd hold his hand and talk to him, not knowing if he could hear me. Sometimes I'd hold back tears. Sometimes they just flowed out. My mind replayed so many memories of us through the years.

When my mom was in the hospital, on Saturdays we would go to a nearby park. They had several public charcoal grills. He'd bring some sort of meat and we'd have a barbeque, just the two of us. He always covered the meat in hickory barbeque sauce and garlic salt, and the meat was always cooked rare. I loved it! Those two ingredients were a constant in his cooking through the years. He would say, "I put garlic salt on everything except my ice cream." To this day, I order all my meat rare and hickory barbeque sauce and garlic salt are now a part of my cooking, too. He also brought his large silver transistor radio along on our outings. I have one photo of us cooking at the park in the rain. We have a blanket covering our heads. His arm is around me and I'm snuggled up next to him with a huge smile on my face. Even the rain couldn't put a damper on our time together.

Though he constantly traveled for work, he always made it to Parent's Weekend for all four years during college. More and more memories just flooded back as I ached inside. The room was quiet except for the clicking sound of the clock on the wall. I was awestruck by what I was about to witness.

He opened his eyes and they were the clearest, purest, shade of green that I'd ever seen. It was like he didn't even know I was in the room with him. He was looking up to the ceiling and started talking. "Wednesday? Oh, okay." Then he picked up his arm and was motioning like he was petting an animal that was sitting on his chest. His dog, Tiger, had passed the year before and he was heartbroken. She was a feisty little terrier mix and he had adored her. I was beyond mesmerized as I watched him seemingly having a conversation with spirits. He looked to the left and said, "Oh, hi," then looked to the right and nodded his head, while he had a huge smile on his face. He then looked up and said, "The 9th? Okay." I'm not quite sure what I was a witness to, but whatever it was, was riveting.

About a week before my dad passed, the clock on the fireplace mantle at my friend, Deb's, house stopped at 2:50. Before he went into a coma on Sunday he looked at me and said, "You are the only thing in this world that means anything to me." Those were his last words to me. At 6:30 in the morning on Wednesday, my phone rang and my heart sank. It was the nursing home telling me that my dad was showing signs of "mottling" and they were confident he would pass that day. I had no idea what mottling was. Once I arrived at his room, I saw his fingertips were turning purple and black. I think I was feeling every emotion possible, simultaneously. I remember trying to memorize everything about his face, his arms, his hands. I kept telling him I loved him in between gut-wrenching sobs. He lifted up his left arm and reached out to me. I took his hand as he took his last breath. It looked like a million shiny sparkles flew out of the top of his head. Then I saw the color drain from his forehead, slowly down his face. I witnessed his transition to another realm. A defining and pivotal moment of my life, hauntingly beautiful and gut-wrenchingly painful--imprecisely woven together.

It was Wednesday, March 9th at 2:50 p.m.

His ashes were interred at Arlington National Cemetery, in the plot along with my mom. He lived 40 years after her passing. Though their time together was brief, it was a love that forever remained in his heart. I've rarely witnessed that powerful a love.

The interment ceremony was incredibly moving. Naval representatives were so kind and gracious. As Taps was played, I felt myself looking at the rows and rows of white grave markers meticulously aligned, just as I did as the 5-year-old child at my mother's grave. He was so proud to know he would be laid to rest at Arlington.

About a month after his death, I made an appointment to see our priest, Father Andy. I described my experience at the moment of my dad's passing. He said what a true gift that was. He explained that it's much more common for a loved one to pass when family just steps out of the room momentarily. He said it's such an intimate and painful moment for those left behind, that the dying will often leave then to spare their loved ones more heartache. What a gift it was for me to be with my dad at the exact moment of his transition, where the veil between the two worlds was lifted.

The more you love, the more difficulty the grieving process. My dad's unconditional love for me never wavered. The joy, laughter and memories now live in my heart each and every day. Not a single day goes by that I don't think of him and smile.

"My father gave me the greatest gift anyone could give another person, he believed in me."
– Jim Valvano

CRAWLING THROUGH THE STORM

*a*s hard as I worked in therapy, I always felt like something else was there. I worked to grieve my mom's death, the dating abuse, the two rapes, and my dad's death. Yet, I had a sadness that wouldn't lift, no matter what joy I was experiencing in my life. I had a career I loved, wonderful friends and an occasional great romantic relationship. Yet, that feeling of self-hatred and worthlessness was constant. I would lose a lot of weight, then sabotage it all by gaining it back, plus more, which fed into my feelings of failure. I couldn't stop drowning my feelings with food.

My half-brother, HB, and I had occasional contact through the years. When I was a senior in college I went to visit him. It was an unnerving experience. I was now 20 years old; he hadn't seen me since I was 5. I do look exactly like our mom, so I figured the reason he was just staring at me for three days was because I looked like her. What I can tell you is every time I had any kind of contact from him, I felt "icky." He literally made my skin crawl. As the years went by, that feeling never left. Things he would say to me on the phone were not what a brother says to his sister. "I love you so much." "I think about you every day." "I wish I could hug and kiss you like I did when you were little," which made me incredibly, incredibly uncomfortable. He kept saying how much he loved me, but he didn't even really know me. It was a strong feeling of revulsion after any type of contact with him. I truly wanted to have a family relationship with him but I just couldn't. For whatever reason, I could just not allow myself to be more involved, or truly include him, in my life. I couldn't get past that "icky" feeling. I kept contact to a bare minimum: birthday calls and Christmas cards. That was enough for me.

One year, I received a Christmas card from him and what he wrote inside infuriated me. "If you accept Jesus Christ as your personal savior, maybe God will allow you to see mom when you die." I felt a raging surge of anger inside me. My face turned red and I immediately ripped the card up. It definitely hit a nerve, and it would continue to down the road—until I understood why.

His wife and I were friends on Facebook. One day, about six years ago, she posted that he was in the hospital with blood clots in his lungs. Something inside told me I had to go see him. The next morning I made the seven-hour drive.

I visited with him and his wife in the hospital; everything was fine. The next morning, I went early to see him because I needed to get on the road to get home. He and I were alone in the room. He started staring at my chest, then made the comment, "Wow, my wife's legs sure don't look like yours!" I felt repulsed but ignored it. I had always suspected that my mother had been molested by her brother. I was talking to HB about it when he looked at me and said, "Well, you said incest between a brother and a sister is okay." He had the most maniacal look on his face. His eyes almost looked demonic. There I was, looking into the face of evil. He then said, "Yeah, I figured if Mom found out, she would cut me up and put me in garbage bags." I felt the air leave the room.

The look on his face is burned into my memory... forever.

I was numb, stunned and I needed to get out of there. I don't remember making the seven-hour drive home. It's only by the grace of God, I didn't have a car accident. When I got home, I locked every door and window. I picked up my cat and just held him, then went into a fetal position on the couch. I couldn't move. I felt dirty. I felt ashamed. I felt anger.

I felt worthless. I felt damaged. I felt sick to my stomach. I think of all our basic needs as human beings, the one to feel safe is at the top of the list. I didn't feel safe and was afraid I never would again.

God love our pets. My cat at the time was Brody and he was such a pocket of joy in my life. I can't tell you how much his unconditional love helped me in my healing. He instinctively knew when something was wrong. He did not leave my side.

The interaction in the hospital room with HB that day turned my whole world upside down. In my soul, I knew nothing would ever be the same. I can describe what unfolded was like a door slowly opening. For 50 years, my mind suppressed the incest. Horrific, buried memories of what he did to me were slowly emerging. I needed to work with Leigh more than ever.

This, THIS was the cancerous tumor at the core of my soul. The ramifications of his sexual abuse subconsciously affected me my entire life.

Of all the challenges I had ever faced, THIS was by far the toughest. I started having nightmares. I wet the bed. I continually didn't feel safe. I didn't want to leave my house. I became hypersensitive. I describe it as feeling like, if someone dropped a paper clip a mile away, I could hear it. I'd leave for work in the morning, then have to go back because I couldn't remember if I turned the coffee pot off. I didn't want to be around anyone. I wanted to be left alone. I wanted to stay awake all night and sleep during the day. The darkness of the night overwhelmed me. However, being a single woman with a mortgage and bills, I had to keep working. I had to keep going. I was responsible for the thirty teachers I supervised. I had to find a way to put my life back together and heal. I knew I was in for the fight of my life. For the second time in my life, I considered suicide, but then I looked at Brody. I couldn't leave him behind. When I adopted him as a kitten, I made a commitment to take care of him until it was his time.

You may think that sounds absurd, but Brody helped save me. He needed me, and I needed his unconditional love. I'm so grateful I didn't give up.

> *"A cat purring on your lap is more healing than*
> *any drug in the world, as the vibrations you are*
> *receiving are of pure love and contentment."*
> *– St. Francis of Assisi*

One day, when I could feel myself start to spiral. I said out loud, "No, you son of a bitch! Your sick actions have unconsciously affected me for 50 years, and I'm not going to give you one more day!" Slowly, very slowly, I began to crawl out of the bowels of hell. Between working with Leigh, and support from two friends who had survived sexual abuse as children, I have emerged a strong survivor. I wanted my power back, and I fought like hell to get it. I completely severed all contact with him. When he was molesting me...I was a precious four-year-old child, and he was a six-foot-five, seventeen-year-old. My dad was working six-hours away from home at the time and only home on the weekends. As our mother was dying in bed in the next room, he was sexually molesting me in the bathroom, in the living room. As a child, I had no control over what was happening, but now as an adult, I did everything I could think of to feel safe. I changed my cell phone number, got an unlisted home phone number, blocked his wife on Facebook and blocked their email address. My best friend and her husband gave me money to have a home security system installed. That precious 4-year-old child was subjected to his control, but this 54-year-old woman was now the one in control.

> *"And one day she realized that she was fierce,*
> *and strong, and full of fire, and not even she*
> *could hold herself back because her passion*
> *burned brighter than her fears."*
> *– Unknown*

I was now able to put all the pieces together. It all now made sense--my aversion to allowing HB in my life, my innate feelings of revulsion after any contact with him, my fear of men as a child, my lifelong feelings of self-hatred and never feeling good enough. *The other horrific experiences I endured were layered on top of the abuse I suffered at his hands.* My little four-year-old mind did what it could to survive, by blocking it from my memory. It's no wonder I had a meltdown during the writing exercise. When I wrote, "Dear Little Gigi. I'll always be here for you." I inadvertently scratched the surface and tapped lightly into that buried trauma.

I'm convinced my father suspected something. He is truly my hero. He got me away from my abuser. My dad passed away in 2005 before the incest with HB came to light, so I never got to tell him that I now know the truth. I loved my dad more than anyone in the world, a gentle giant with that quick Irish wit and a heart the size of Texas.

In a seven-month time period, three cataclysmic events erupted:

Month one, I found out Jake passed away. Month four, the unmasking of the buried incest with HB emerged. Month seven, my abusive high school ex-boyfriend made major threats to me.

I thought I had forgiven my abusive high school ex and he truly seemed to have changed. My friends thought it was pretty remarkable that I allowed him in my life after what he put me through in high school. It's what I thought I was supposed to do. We did occasionally spend time together. He could be great company. A very close friend who had witnessed his treatment of me during those years asked me, "Why would you want to be friends with your abuser?" That really struck me, and she was right. I soon got to a point where I made a decision to just let the friendship go.

I was not prepared for his reaction. I started receiving the vilest and threatening emails and phone calls--threatening to contact my boss and have me fired, threatening to physically come after me. His unbelievable demeaning messages and emails were aimed at completely destroying me. This man who I thought had changed, had not. He was the same abuser from 40 years ago, but even worse.

I went to my local police station because I wanted to know if there was something I could do to make him stop. I explained to the officer what was going on. He looked at me and smugly said, "Yeah, but what did you do?" I was shocked! Was he kidding me? He was apparently inferring I had done something to cause this. No wonder victims are hesitant to go to law enforcement. It was hard to accept his reaction. As that 18-year-old rape victim in college, I would have crumbled if I had gone to the police and had this type of response.

This situation alone would have been bad enough, but the fact that it happened only three months after the uncovering of the incest, was more than I could handle. My fear and anxiety were beyond exacerbated.

Thank God for Leigh. I worked harder than I ever had in my life. I went to my doctor and explained what had happened, and she cried with me. I was diagnosed with clinical depression and started medication. I was literally dying inside and hope was something I had given up on.

This was the darkest time period I had ever experienced, but I could hear my dad's words, "You just keep going."

It's interesting when gifts present themselves disguised as opportunities. About nine months after everything exploded, I was asked to fill in to do a presentation on mandated child abuse reporting. My first reaction was "No way." But then I decided, I did, in fact, need to do this. It was two half-day sessions for about 140 people and child sexual abuse was included in the information. At the end of the second session, a mother and daughter walked up to me. The mother said, "My daughter's abuser, who was a family member, did not spend one night in jail." Without even thinking, out of my mouth came, "Neither did mine." She looked shocked and I think I shocked myself when I said it. But you know what? It felt great, to be honest. I had no shame. I spoke my truth. The opportunity to do that presentation was truly a gift. It showed me I was stronger than I gave myself credit for.

The horrific truth of what my mind buried for 50 years was the demon I was never able to reach. For years, it was like putting a band-aid on a tumor. Slowly, very slowly, Leigh helped me through all of it. She was my lifeline. My sessions with her kept me going forward. One day I was so tired, and ready to just quit. I remember saying out loud to God, "Either take me or heal me, I can't stay like this any longer." To be honest, I didn't care which one He chose.

Apparently, He had plans for me to not only heal and emerge stronger but to be a messenger of hope to other survivors who, like me, didn't think healing was possible.

I've said it before, but healing is such a process, such a journey, and it looks different for everyone. It doesn't happen in a straight line. It wasn't until I truly believed deep inside myself, that more than anything, I DESERVED to heal. I was worth the journey to get there.

Honoring my personal boundaries, in itself, was huge for me. Learning how to say no may sound simple, but it took practice for me to learn to do what was best for me. Listen to your inner voice. YOUR opinions and feelings matter. The more you have the opportunity to practice this, the easier it becomes. Trust me, it feels great!

I had to learn what self-care was. I love this saying by Lalah Delia: "Self-care is how you take your power back." I spent a lifetime of punishing myself with food and over-ate in an attempt to avoid feeling anything. I now feel so much better physically when I avoid refined sugars, white flour products and processed foods. I was so uncomfortable allowing myself to truly feel any painful emotions. I've learned it's normal to feel cranky, sad and bitchy at times. It's important to nourish your body with healthy foods. Had I been able to do that earlier, I could have avoided developing Type 2 diabetes. Self-care includes any activity you do that nourishes your mental, emotional and physical health. I began to think of it as making choices for my overall long term wellness. Another thing I did was releasing toxic friendships. I used to think that once someone was in your life, they would be there forever. I learned that there are some relationships that just run their course and that's okay.

Now here's a moment of awakening that I finally had: the particular number on the scale on any given day does not determine my value as a human being. You may be thinking, "Well of course it doesn't." But, those decades of an eating disorder, self-hatred, and my own body-shaming was a major hurdle to conquer. For years and years, I thought being thin equated to love and happiness. At my thinnest weight, I was wearing a size 31x34 Levi jean, but I was miserable. I had to learn how to eat to live, not live to eat. I am now a full-figured, curvy, 60-year-old woman, who loves and appreciates her body more now than any other point in her life. It's not about wearing a certain size; it's about your health. Even after all I've worked to heal, I'm cognizant that when I'm feeling an uncomfortable emotion, I still want to run to food. Now, when I have a bad food day, I no longer beat myself up. I just start over.

I had boyfriends who were critical of my weight. Now I would not give any man the time of day who would be so disrespectful. That's another benefit of healing, you are able to recognize what you will and will not tolerate in your life. It feels damn good!

I had to learn what self-love was. I spent years abusing and punishing myself. I internalized all the trauma and turned it inward against myself. With Leigh's help, I processed through each traumatic event. I soon realized that each baby step I took towards having confidence and a positive view of myself was slowly coming together. I was finally seeing my worth and value as a woman and learning to really love Gigi for who she is. I am a valuable and worthy person.

I know I have already said this, but I would not be where I am today without Leigh's help. I can't stress enough how important having the right therapist has made all the difference. I was incredibly blessed that I clicked with the first one I went to. I have heard people say, "Therapy didn't work for me." To me, that means they had not found the right one. Maybe the first one you try isn't right, keep looking. Your therapist will guide you to find your own answers and your own empowerment.

I also credit my tough, fighting-Irish spirit for eventually kicking in. There again, I could hear my dad, "No matter what, just keep going." Oh, Big John, you are so right.

> *"Your trauma is valid. Even if other people have experienced 'worse.' Even if someone else who went through the same experience doesn't feel debilitated by it. Even if it 'could have been avoided.' Even if it happened a long time ago. Even if no one knows. Your trauma is real and valid and you deserve a space to talk about it. It isn't desperate or pathetic or attention-seeking. It's self-care. It's inconceivably brave. And regardless of the magnitude of your struggle, you're allowed to take care of yourself by processing and unloading some of the pain you carry. Your pain matters. Your experience matters. And your healing matters. Nothing and no one can take that away."*
>
> *– Daniell Koepke*

I've been asked if I have forgiven each of these four men. I honestly can't say I can use the word "forgive" because to me that implies I excuse their behavior. But what I will say is, they no longer have any power over me. The opposite of love is not hate, it's indifference. They now mean nothing to me. They are irrelevant. I don't care if they win the Nobel Prize or drop dead. That's been the freedom for me.

> *"Healing doesn't mean the damage never existed.*
> *It means the damage no longer controls our lives."*
> – Unknown

I have no doubt that each of them was wrestling with their own hidden demons, but that did not give them the right to project their violence and abuse onto me. The stain is on their soul, not mine.

I didn't know if I'd ever be able to get over what I had endured. I didn't know if it was possible to heal. I want every survivor to know it is possible and you are so worth it. Believe in yourself and that you deserve it.

I dug deep into my soul and discovered that my true power comes from within.

> *"You've always had the Power my dear,*
> *you just had to learn it for yourself."*
> – Glinda, The Wonderful Wizard of Oz

Sharing the Joy Within

*"There is no force equal to a woman
determined to rise."*
– W.E.B. DuBois

I will say this again to the four men who could have permanently destroyed me: you are irrelevant.

Let's review some pretty wonderful events. During my career in special education, I had so many positive and fulfilling experiences, so many pockets of joy. Along with being nominated for the "Outstanding Young Educator Award," I was nominated for "Educator of the Year" at the State Vision Conference. I presented at a state conference for Non-Public School Administrators. I sat on a panel at the state conference for Gifted Education. I taught as an adjunct instructor at the university I graduated from.

I retired from the field of special education after thirty-two years. It was an incredible experience, but it was time to move on.

In April 2017, I spoke at "Take Back the Night" in the town in which I grew up. I shared my story. I spoke my truth. The love in the room that night, and the connections that were made, were powerful. Several people approached me afterward and asked me if I was a national speaker. I was flattered but actually laughed. As I was driving home, I thought to myself, Maybe this was something I could do on a regular basis to help survivors. The opportunity I had that night marked the beginning of my new passion and mission—I could feel it in my soul. I had no idea where to start or what to do but I reached out and started making contacts.

"Follow your passion.
It will lead you to your purpose."
– Oprah Winfrey

I now share my journey of healing, and offer a message of hope, as a Volunteer Speaker of "Resilient Voices", through OVA (Office of Victim Advocate). I am also a member of the Speakers Bureau for RAINN (Rape, Abuse and Incest National Network).

I often think how having the opportunity to hear someone speak who was also a survivor would have really helped me. I felt so alone when I was trying to heal. I am now completely invested in being an example to those who have lost hope. My message is adamant: **No one** has the right to extinguish the light that shines within you.

When I was a child, my grandmother told me I should always wear something red because it was my color. All these years later, I have put her advice to good use. Each time I have the opportunity to speak, I wear red. To me, red represents power and passion but not romantic passion. It's the passion to heal, the passion to get on the other side of the pain and to celebrate who I am and what I have overcome.

"You weren't made to replicate, obey or stand
in the shadow of another person.
You were made to stand in your own power
and find the truth in your Soul."
– Lonerwolf

I continue to be asked to share my story at various events and classes, including "Impact of Crime Classes" within prisons across Pennsylvania and "Take Back the Night" events. Each is an opportunity to encourage other survivors. There was a purpose for all the traumatic events I had experienced. What a gift this is. I've looked into the eyes of survivors who have told me they wish they could be where I am in my healing. My answer is always, "You can be. You deserve to heal and take your power back. I am a walking, breathing, living example of what it possible!"

Speaking in the prisons was never anything I saw myself doing.

The very first time I spoke in a prison was as a guest speaker during "Crime Victims' Rights Week." There sat over a hundred inmates from the general population and several staff members. I had no idea the audience would be so large. My heart was racing. I took a deep breath when I took the microphone to speak. I had no notes in front of me. I spoke from my heart.

As I looked in the faces of those inmates, I wondered how many of them had also been sexually assaulted. Statistics support that one in six males will be sexually assaulted by the time they are 18-years-old. No doubt there were many survivors in the audience.

Several of them came up to me afterward to speak with me. One man looked at me and said, "I could have never done what you just did." I could tell by the look in his eyes, he was a survivor. Another man said, "My mom went through some of the same things you did. Do you have any advice for her?" Another inmate said, "What you just shared really moved me. I used to sell crack and took advantage of a lot of women. Do you think if I apologized when I get out of here that it would matter?" Several others told me they just wanted to thank me for sharing my story and for being so brave.

However, it was the conversation with one specific inmate that I wasn't expecting. He shared with me that he was serving a life sentence for killing the man who raped his girlfriend. He looked to only be in his early 30s. He was a gifted artist and was currently trying to distribute a symbol that he designed for sexual assault awareness. He shared with me that he has sent it to several places in the hopes to market it, but because he is an inmate, no one was interested.

I thought a lot about my conversation with this young man

while I was driving home. I truly understood the anger he felt when his girlfriend was raped. The one difference between that young man and myself was the fact he acted on his anger and rage while I did not.

Once the feeling of shock from the reality of the incest subsided, my emotions morphed to pure anger and rage. I dreamed of revenge. I never in my life had such pure hatred for another human being. I wanted him to suffer. I wanted him to pay for what he did to me. He destroyed my chance for any type of normalcy during childhood. He is the reason I've struggled with intimacy issues. What he did to me will be with me for the rest of my life. The false Christian who hid behind his religion tried to make me think I said the incest was okay. The dark thoughts I had regarding what I felt would be just punishment for him, scared me. I leaned on Leigh and she was able to help me process through it all. This portion of my healing journey was *extremely* difficult. The mask he wears for the world to see does not adequately represent who he truly is. He can project his image of being the pious Christian to the world but I know the truth. He is a monster. Do I think evil walks the earth? Yes, yes I do. I looked into its face that day in the hospital.

When I speak at the "Impact of Crime Classes," the groups are not as large, only about 20 inmates. I can tell by the expressions on their faces who is really listening and who would like me to go away. In one particular class, I was caught off guard by a question. I had an uncomfortable feeling about one inmate in the back of the room.

He looked at me and said, "I can understand why you want to speak to young women, but why do you want to speak to men? And, are you able to have relations with men now?" I heard a few gasps from the other inmates, while one man in the front let out a sigh of disgust. This particular moment reminded me of being a classroom teacher, who has that one student that will challenge you as the other students in the class are staring at you, waiting for your reaction.

I thought to myself, "Okay, here we go."

My response went something like this...

"This class is called 'Impact of Crime.' I am a living, breathing example to show the ramifications of how what I have endured has affected me. I consider myself one of the lucky ones because I had the proper treatment and support to point me towards healing. Other survivors are not so lucky. I speak to both male and female survivors to offer hope and to let them know what's possible. I speak to perpetrators to remind them that their actions leave a lifetime of permanent scarring."

This perpetrator then looked like he had been knocked down a peg and did not ask any further questions.

I did not address his question regarding my "relations" with men, because I had a gut feeling he was looking for intimate details. His complete inappropriateness did not warrant a response.

Feedback from the classes has been positive. Many of the inmates said that what I shared with them really made them look at things differently. Each time I speak to groups within the prisons, I feel I am there to represent the voices of all survivors who have not had the chance to be heard.

I had the opportunity to speak at a residential treatment facility for adolescent females. Their teacher, Cindy, is an amazing woman and educator. After she heard me speak she said to me, "I always wondered what the sadness was behind your eyes." Wow, she was able to pick up on what I thought I had done such a good job of hiding from the world.

When I left that afternoon, she had each of the girls write a reflection. I had no idea of this writing activity, but a few days later she gave those reflections to me. I was sitting at my dining room table reading them and was completely overwhelmed with emotion. These young women are between the ages of thirteen to eighteen. As I was reading them, my cat, Louie, jumped up on the table and just nuzzled into me as if to comfort me.

> *"We may have pets, but when it comes to*
> *unconditional love, they are the masters."*
> *– Donald L. Hicks*

Animals so easily give unconditional love. Why is it so hard for humans?

The honesty those young women expressed in those reflections was so raw. They really heard my message. My hope is that when they leave this facility and go on with their lives, they will remember our afternoon together and remember they can and deserve to heal.

Here are a couple examples from all the reflections;

"Thank you for telling me that what happened to me wasn't my fault, and thank you for showing me what a strong woman looks like—I've never seen one."

"When I think of what happened to me, Miss Gigi said the stain is on their soul, not mine."

"I thought what she told us was very sad and very powerful. Sad because of the struggles she went through, and powerful because of the person she has become. She had a lot of kind and empowering words for us and told us that no one has the right to extinguish the light that shines within us. I want to have that feeling of peace within myself that she does. She made me realize that what happened to me was not my fault and I am worth so much more than what has been done to me, and with a little love and understanding, I can overcome anything."

Looking at the precious faces of these young women, knowing what some of them had already survived, was harrowing. To think I almost gave up--almost took my life twice. Had I gone through with it, I would never have known the joy of what true healing feels like, nor had this phenomenal opportunity to have a positive impact on survivors.

I do not refer to myself as a victim. I am a survivor. When those traumatic events were happening to me, I was being victimized. But because of sheer determination, and Leigh's guidance, I learned how to take back my power. If I had allowed myself to stay stuck and allowed what happened to me to keep me stuck, and consequently not worked towards healing, they would have won. They did not deserve to win--I did.

> *"She fell*
> *She crashed*
> *She broke*
> *She cried*
> *She crawled*
> *She hurt*
> *She surrendered*
> *And then...*
> *She rose again"*
> *– Nausicaa Twila*

To date, I have had the opportunity to speak in one, female-only prison. There were about 20 of us in a small classroom. After I shared my story, many of them opened up and shared gut-wrenching life experiences. Many of them are incarcerated, not because they committed a horrific crime, but because they were with someone who did. Most were survivors of domestic abuse and/or rape. Many chose a detrimental coping mechanism just to survive. One of the inmates looked at me and asked, "When you leave here, what are you going to tell your friends about us?" I replied, "That you're all awesome." Every single woman in that room smiled.

My afternoon with these women left an indelible impression on me. I wanted to stay longer and continue to talk with them. Leaving the prison, I drove down the long road to the main highway. I kept looking in my rearview mirror staring at the white dome on the main building and the barbed wire everywhere. As this slowly began to fade from view, my eyes started to tear up and I felt such a sadness. I was able to get in my car and drive away. Many of those who were in that room with me will only be able to leave in a hearse.

If you are reading this and you're not sure you can heal--trust me when I tell you that you can. For the first time in my life, I have that inner peace that I constantly yearned for. Happiness doesn't come from something outside of you; it doesn't come from another person. It comes from within. I know what it's like to have lost hope. But please, please know there is always hope. It took me a long time to get to where I am today. There is support available. Please reach out if you are struggling. I promise you, it does get better.

I now wake up each morning and thank God for everything I have. Those horrible experiences I survived by those four men--did... not... break... me. This tough Irish gal is here to tell you that despite whatever you have gone through, those pockets of joy in your life that touch your soul and bring you peace are what matters.

A couple of months ago, I had an experience validating that healing is an ongoing process.

I was called for jury selection. Of course, you have no idea what kind of case you will be involved in. As the charges for this defendant were being read, I felt myself start to tremble, and the room closing in on me. What was described was a horrific account of dating violence. It had been a very long time since something would trigger me, sending me into the hell of panic and anxiety.

At one point when the attorneys were asking the potential jurors questions, the question was, "Does anyone here think they would not be able to be impartial in this case due to moral, ethical or religious beliefs?" I knew I had a split second to either speak up or keep my mouth shut.

I raised my hand, had to stand up and give my name and juror number. My voice was cracking and I was trembling but I got the words out: "I am a survivor and I do not believe I would be able to be impartial in this case. I'm sorry." As I looked at the defendant who had such anger in his eyes, it felt like I was looking at each of the four men who subjected me to their violence and evil. What came next was completely unexpected and left a tender mark on my soul. The judge said, "Miss Kilroe, you have absolutely nothing to be sorry about. I appreciate your candor." I saw a look of compassion on his face, a look I'll never forget. He asked both attorneys if they had any objection to me being stricken from the list. Neither objected and I was able to leave.

I couldn't get out of the courthouse fast enough. I just wanted to get home, in my home where I feel safe.

I was parked in a parking garage and once I finally found my car, I had a terrible time getting out. When you are overwhelmed by painful emotions, sometimes it makes you feel scattered, like you can't ground yourself. While I tried to exit, I kept following the arrow that took me to the next level up. I was just a mess, swearing up a storm and making the same wrong turns for what felt like hours.

Once home, I was able to calm myself down. Deep breaths, self-talk, running my hand under the kitchen faucet, feeling the water...all helped to ground me and bring me back. I picked up my cat, Louie, and kissed his face about 100 times. He was just precious, snuggled into me and purring loudly. I was ok - I survived the trigger, the unexpected boulder in the road that smacked me in the face. This demon from the past unexpectedly emerged momentarily, but I knocked the beast away and claimed my victory.

Healing is indeed a journey, a process. Triggers are still possible even after a long and thorough journey of healing, but they won't destroy you. If anything, they show you how far you have come.

"Avoiding your triggers isn't healing.
Healing happens when you're triggered

and you're able to move through the pain,
the pattern, and the story—
and walk your way to a different ending."
– Vienna Pharaon

A week later I wrote and sent a thank you note to the judge. I wanted him to know how much I appreciated his kindness.

The statistics I have seen are horrifying:

One in three girls and one in six boys will be sexually abused before they turn 18-years-old.

Thirty-three percent of adolescents in America are victim to sexual, physical, verbal or emotional dating abuse.

About one in four young women will be sexually assaulted across our nation's college campuses, with only twenty percent being reported.

Here I am—a statistic in each of those three categories.

We are survivors. We will always be survivors. But those experiences don't define who we are, they just become woven into the tapestries of our lives. Find your passions--music, art, sports--whatever it is that brings you joy. In my healing work, I discovered I am happiest when I am doing something creative. I made a huge sun/moon stained glass piece that now hangs in my breezeway. I've gathered materials and started watching YouTube videos on how to create mixed media glass bottles. The chance to tap into my creativity has been so healing for me. Spending time with my goddaughter is priceless. Since I was never able to have children of my own, the love and bond between us brings me so much joy. Laughing so hard with friends that I'm crying--such joy! My home is filled with candles and little white lights. These are very centering and calming to me. I also never take anyone or anything for granted.

*"You gain strength, courage and confidence by
every experience in which you really stop and
look fear in the face. You are able to say to yourself,
I lived through this horror. I can take the next thing
that comes along. You must do the thing
you think you cannot do."*

– Eleanor Roosevelt

In the long hallway in my home, I have created a "Gallery of Joy." I went through all my photo albums and pulled out 100 of my favorites. It's a combination of family, ancestors and friends. I had each printed in different sizes all in black and white and put them in black frames with white matting. Photos, and the joys of the memories they contain, have always been so important to me. It's wonderful to see them all together each time I walk down the hall. The greatest concrete visual I have, spanning my lifetime to date, is of my pockets of joy.

My favorite quote of all time is by Maya Angelou and it is how I now live my life:

*"My mission in life is not merely to survive, but
to thrive; and to do so with some passion, some
compassion, some humor, and some style."*

Never ever, ever underestimate random acts of kindness. We never know what someone is going through. The simplest gesture of kindness you make to another human being can mean all the difference in the world. I often think of Jimmy, that precious little guy from the day camp. He'll never know how his words to me touched my soul and led me to a 32-year career in special education.

Before my gram passed she said, "But you're not settled!" Which meant, "But you're not married!" The expectation of her time period was to get married and have children. For the longest time, I allowed that to make me feel less than because it wasn't in the cards for me.

I no longer believe I'm less than, not worthy, damaged or broken. I believe I'm right where I'm supposed to me. My journey of growth and healing is the hardest thing I've ever done but by far the most rewarding. What an amazing road is now in front of me.

> *"The only way to do great work is*
> *to love what you do. If you haven't*
> *found it yet, keep looking. Don't settle.*
> *As with all matters of the heart,*
> *you'll know when you find it."*
> *– Steve Jobs*

Each time I have the opportunity to share my story and meet other survivors, something incredible happens. We enter the room as strangers, but by the end of our time together our souls have somehow gently connected without judgment. Our present circumstances are not important. Whether you are an inmate, an adolescent, a college student, middle-aged or elderly, we are all human beings who have somehow been violated. The age range of those I've spoken to has spanned from 13 to 73. To be able to express warmth and compassion towards each other is powerful. To be able to witness these interactions has been such a gift.

Yes, I've survived hell. But each stop and start, every success and failure, have all shaped me into the strong, content, grateful woman I am today. All the years I spent focusing on the outside in search of happiness, I now realize I was looking in the wrong place. If I wasn't busy changing my hair color or trying a fad diet, I was buying earrings or skincare products, or expecting a man to be my answer. I didn't know how to fill that hole or calm that ache deep inside my soul. My bathroom shelves looked like the skincare counter at Macy's. One day, my friend Rich walked into my bathroom and said, "Jesus Christ, it looks like Cleopatra's tomb in here!"

Peace, joy and happiness all come from within. It wasn't

until I hit all the demons from my past head-on, that I realized I deserved so much more. I have finally replaced self-hatred with self-love.

Each time I share my story, more and more of the shame I've carried is chipped away. I have finally found my voice, and I've now been given this extraordinary opportunity to help others find theirs.

> *"What lies behind us and what lies before us*
> *are tiny matters compared to what lies within us."*
> *– Ralph Waldo Emerson*

I want you to remember this. If you ever feel alone, like no one could possibly understand what you are going through or what you are feeling, I want YOU to know I'm with you, holding YOUR hand... looking YOU dead in the eyes... saying to YOU the precious words of Jimmy, the day camper: I like you!

RESOURCES

National Sexual Assault Hotline
1-800-656-4673, available 24/7

National Dating Abuse Helpline
www.loveisrespect.org, 1-866-331-9474

National Sexual Violence Resource Center
www.NSVRC.org, 1-877-739-3895

Rape, Abuse & Incest National Network (RAINN)
www.RAINN.org, 1-800-656-HOPE (4673)

Support for Male Survivors
www.1in6.org, 1-800-656-HOPE (4673)

Survivors of Incest Anonymous
www.siawso.org, 1-877-742-9761

Gigi Kilroe earned her BS in Early Childhood Education, MS in Exceptional Persons and Special Education Supervisory Certification from Bloomsburg University. She retired after a career of 32 years in the field of special education; she worked nine years as a special education teacher and then 23 years as a special education supervisor. Working with students with special needs was her passion.

Once a victim, who has since emerged a strong survivor, Gigi's passion is now to share her journey of healing and, more importantly, her message of hope to survivors of all ages.

Gigi is now a speaker for Resilient Voices out of the Office of Victim Advocate in Harrisburg, PA, a member of The Crime Victim Alliance of PA, and a member of the Speakers Bureau for RAINN (Rape, Abuse & Incest National Network). She is committed to sharing her journey as an example to those who need to know; no matter what you have endured, you deserve to heal and take your power back.